Skill Qualification and Turbulence in the Army National Guard and Army Reserve

Richard Buddin, David W. Grissmer

Prepared for the
Assistant Secretary of Defense (Reserve Affairs)

National Defense Research Institute

PREFACE

Improving the personnel and training readiness of Selected Reserve units requires, among other things, the identification of problems in meeting readiness goals, the causes of these problems, and likely solutions. This report addresses the issue of individual job training in the Army National Guard and Army Reserve. For several reasons, a significant proportion of reservists in units are not even minimally qualified in their assigned jobs. These reasons include the large share of prior-service personnel requiring retraining, the large number of reservists who change units and jobs over their career, and forces retraining required when the force structure changes or is modernized. This research has established a job tracking system for reservists and used that system to measure job qualification levels in different units and jobs. It has also measured the frequency of assigned job changes and provided evidence on the causes of such changes. Finally, it has measured average retraining times for reservists changing jobs.

This research on reserve training readiness issues is sponsored by the Office of the Assistant Secretary of Defense (Reserve Affairs). The research is conducted by the Defense Manpower Research Center, part of RAND's National Defense Research Institute, a federally funded research and development center sponsored by the Office of the Secretary of Defense and the Joint Staff.

CONTENTS

FIGURES

TABLES

SUMMARY

BACKGROUND

Most reserve units mobilized for Operation Desert Storm needed personnel assigned from outside the unit prior to deployment. These personnel filled positions that were either vacant or held by individuals who were not job qualified. These positions could not be filled by mobilizing individual reservists from other units because by law only reserve units and not individual reservists can be mobilized. A variety of "cross-leveling" methods were used for filling these units. Volunteers with the appropriate qualifications from other units often joined units prior to mobilization, or individuals were involuntarily transferred prior to mobilization. In some cases, individuals from the active force or Individual Ready Reserve (IRR) were assigned after mobilization.

Ideally, reserve units in peacetime should be fully manned with individuals who are qualified for their jobs and who have trained together. This would avoid the delays associated with cross-leveling and the problems of integrating new personnel into existing units. It would avoid any degradation in performance that might occur if personnel have not trained together. Filling all positions with trained personnel would also improve peacetime unit training, which can be affected by numerous vacancies and untrained personnel.

The problems of unfilled unit positions and unqualified personnel are much less serious for active units. The active force can fill vacancies by assigning *any* trained soldier to *any* unit by transferring the individual to the unit location. This allows the active Army to quickly fill unit vacancies with trained personnel and to continuously maintain high-priority units at full manning with qualified personnel. Since reservists cannot be geographically relocated, vacancies are filled through voluntary transfers between nearby units or recruiting new personnel from the geographical area to fill the position.

New training for the vacant position is usually required whether the position is filled by transferring or newly recruited personnel. Transferring personnel may need to be retrained because the few units nearby often have different missions. Newly recruited non-prior-service personnel all require training and newly recruited prior-service personnel need retraining in a majority of cases because their active-duty primary job does not match the needs of the unit. The process of recruiting or retraining in the reserve forces can take from four months to over a year, and during this period the position is held for the person being trained and thus is not filled by a qualified person. This is the major reason that reserve units can have large numbers of positions that upon mobilization need to be filled by cross-leveling.

This problem cannot easily be solved efficiently by starting recruiting and retraining earlier (a training pipeline) based on predictions of which positions are going to be vacant. Predictions can be statistically accurate only if there are a large number of positions requiring similar job training and historical attrition patterns in these skills have understandable trends. The active force can assign individuals emerging from the training pipeline to any unit, and it can estimate training requirements by job category based on the number of positions with similar jobs and pay grades in the entire force. Thus if the active Army has a requirement for 30,000 E4 infantrymen, it can estimate attrition patterns from these positions accurately and have trained personnel ready to fill positions anywhere they occur.

This process cannot work for reserve forces because it depends on being able to assign newly trained personnel to any unit where vacancies occur. For reserve units, a training pipeline would have to be established for each unit. Since typical reserve units have 50 to 150 positions spread across many different jobs and pay grades, attrition for specific groups of similar positions cannot be accurately predicted. Attempting to create a pipeline of trained individuals for each reserve unit would result in significant overmanning of reserve units and retraining of personnel when expected positions do not open up. Since creating pipelines for each unit is inefficient, other policies that attempt to reduce the level of unqualified personnel must be explored. In assessing these policies, it is important to distinguish between those that make the problem more visible and those that attempt to solve the problem. Recent legislation would make the problem more visible but not solve the problem.

Title XI[1] requires Army National Guard (ARNG) units to report unit strength based on qualified personnel only. Previously, reserve unit strength included both trained and untrained personnel for a position. This meant that a reserve unit could appear fully manned but still have 20 to 30 percent of its personnel unqualified. Unit manning statistics for active units automatically include only qualified personnel since only trained personnel are assigned to unit positions. Thus, active and reserve forces were often compared using inaccurate measures. This discrepancy could cause models of wartime outcomes and sustainability to overestimate reserve capability. Cost comparisons of active and reserve forces would make reserve forces look too inexpensive, and a force mix with too many reserve units could result. Finally, too few training resources would be allocated to reserve units.

The new reporting structure should solve these problems. However, it is important to realize that the new reporting methods will not solve the problem of unqualified personnel—only raise its visibility and allow for more accurate data in decisionmaking. This report addresses the continuing problem of individuals not job qualified in Army Reserve (USAR) and ARNG units.

PURPOSE OF THE REPORT

This report explores the extent of and causes for enlisted personnel lacking military occupational specialty (MOS) qualification in their assigned duty MOS, and suggests policy initiatives to help remedy

---

[1]*National Defense Authorization Act for Fiscal Year 1993*, U.S. Congress, House report 102–966, 1992.

this problem. Untrained personnel can arise from three sources. Nonprior-service individuals awaiting or undergoing initial training are currently counted as unit members, but have not yet qualified in an initial MOS. The second source of MOS unqualified individuals is prior-service accessions needing retraining in an MOS different from their active-duty MOS. The third source of unqualified individuals is reservists undergoing retraining at some career point after initial training.

In this report we concentrate on the latter two sources of unqualified personnel: entering prior-service personnel and reservists undergoing retraining. These individuals are in pay grades E3 to E9 and are not currently MOS qualified. This group comprises about three-fourths of assigned individuals who are not MOS qualified. This report answers several questions regarding job qualification and retraining in the Army Guard and Army Reserve. They include:

- What are job qualification levels among E3 to E9 and how do these qualification levels differ across job types, types of units, and components?

- Do early deploying units have higher job qualification levels than later deploying units?

- How frequently do individuals retrain and how does this vary across units and job types?

- How quickly do individuals requalify in new jobs?

- How does retraining time vary across units and job types?

- What factors determine the level of job qualification and retraining?

- How much of retraining can be attributed to reservists relocating because of civilian job changes?

APPROACH

To identify the causes of retraining and address the above questions, we developed a job tracking system for each reservist that can identify his or her reserve unit and its characteristics, the status of current jobs, and changes in assigned jobs and associate these changes with concurrent changes in units, promotion, and civilian home of record. We have used three data sources and obtained information on approximately 25,000 individuals. We constructed a longitudinal data file for reservists and analyzed data from June 1986 to September 1987. This period serves as a baseline for testing the models and for establishing trends and causes for ongoing analysis of more recent data. Analysis of more recent data is continuing.

The data allow us to determine changes in primary and duty MOS as well as unit changes and geographical migration for each reservist in the file. We can also estimate MOS qualification levels for different MOS and units at two points in time and determine duty reassignments during that 15-month period. We have estimated a recursive logit model that links qualification levels at two points in time and the job turbulence during the period into a unified framework. We estimate and present results from three equations describing:

- Job qualification in June 1986,

- Job changes between June 1986 and September 1987,

- Qualification in September 1987.

RESULTS

Our analysis of the various populations of reservists leads to several major conclusions:

- Although the percentages vary by subcategory, units in the ARNG and USAR usually have 20 to 30 percent of positions filled by not-yet-qualified soldiers who would not be deployable.

- Although the ARNG has higher levels of job qualification than the USAR, the differences appear to be attributable to the different job mix and not to any difference in policy or environment in the two components.

- A high degree of turbulence caused by personnel who change units and jobs is an important factor contributing to the low levels of qualification. Only 62 percent of ARNG personnel and 56 percent of USAR personnel remain in the same unit and job over 18 months.

- Only a small proportion of unit changes are attributable to civilian job changes requiring geographical relocation, but rather seem to be motivated by individual desire for different jobs or promotion opportunity.

- About 50 to 60 percent of entering prior-service reservists need retraining to MOS different from their active-duty skills.

- Retraining reservists in a new MOS takes a long time—nine to ten months on the average and longer for combat jobs.

MOS Qualification

Approximately 16 percent of E3 to E9 personnel in the Guard and 25 percent of Army Reserve personnel were not qualified in June 1986. When E1 and E2 personnel are added to this figure, the overall percentage of personnel not qualified is between 20 and 30 percent. The rates of E3 to E9 personnel not qualified are much higher for prior-service personnel and those in noncombat jobs. Nonprior-service personnel had unqualified rates in the Guard and Reserve of 12 percent and 20 percent, respectively, compared with 23 and 29 percent for prior-service personnel. Combat jobs in the Guard had unqualified rates of only 8 percent compared with 25 percent for noncombat technical jobs and 19 percent for noncombat nontechnical jobs. In the Reserve, combat jobs had only slightly lower unqualified rates of 22 percent compared with 26 percent for technical and 25 percent for nontechnical jobs.

While the Guard has lower levels of unqualified personnel, most of this difference is attributable to the different mix of jobs in the two components. The Guard has significantly more combat jobs, and these tend to have significantly lower rates of job turbulence and levels of unqualified personnel. The level of unqualified personnel among non-combat jobs is higher than for combat jobs and about the same in both components.

Changing Jobs and Units

Reservists change jobs frequently. We find that 21 percent of E3 to E9 personnel in the Guard change jobs over the 15-month period, as do 32 percent of the Army Reserve. Job switching is less frequent from combat jobs, which explains their higher level of job qualification. The high rate of job switching means that the original Initial Active-Duty Training (IADT) investment from previous active MOS is rapidly lost. After five years in the Army Reserve, only one-half of nonprior-service enlistees are in their original IADT MOS. For prior-service personnel, only about 40 to 50 percent serve in jobs matching their active-duty MOS, and after five years, only 20 percent of reservists are in their original active-duty MOS.

Most job switching occurs in conjunction with unit switching. Unit switching is not primarily a result of geographical migration of reservists, but is rather voluntary switching among local units. Eighty percent of unit switches occur among units less than 50 miles apart. Over 80 percent of reservists have a choice of ten or more units within 50 miles of their home for unit changes. Strong evidence in the Guard indicates that switching is driven primarily by a desire for promotion, whereas in the Army Reserve changing to more desirable jobs may play an important role.

Retraining

We have developed an estimate of the average retraining times for reservists by tracking individuals who changed duty MOS (DMOS) and either did or did not requalify by the end of the 15-month period. Improved data that track individuals over longer time periods would considerably improve these estimates. The present estimates show average retraining times of between nine and ten months for both the Guard and Reserve. However, combat jobs take considerably longer to retrain than noncombat skills. Combat skills took 12 to 13 months, whereas noncombat skills took six to nine months. In the active force, combat jobs have the shortest training times. The difference might be explained by the need for field training and testing, and the fact that Reserve combat units go to the field only four to six times a year. Or, combat retraining may be more structured and tighter quality control exercised for a variety of reasons—some related to risk of personnel injury or equipment damage.

RECOMMENDATIONS

Our recommendations include the following:

- Change prior-service bonus policies to reward matching active-duty MOS and reserve DMOS at entry and job longevity once in the reserve components.

- Initiate supplementary proficiency pay for reservists that can be variable across units and jobs that would pay reservists for the length of time in a job.

- Make "simple" modifications to the reserve pay table to extend or increase longevity increments and reduce promotion incentives.

- Prudently change the Modified Tables of Organization and Equipment (MTOE) to make higher grade progression possible within job categories that are difficult to fill or require longer training times.

- Establish minimum job tenure periods after training and retraining to recoup training investment.

- Regulate intercomponent and interunit transfers to protect training investment.

ACKNOWLEDGMENTS

We are grateful to Brigadier General Carl Morin, the Deputy Assistant Secretary of Defense for Readiness and Training in the Office of the Assistant Secretary of Defense for Reserve Affairs, for his encouragement and support of this research. Libby Hinson, formerly of RAND, provided critical assistance in acquiring data and collecting background information from visits with reserve units. Jerry Sollinger of RAND improved the structure and clarity of the report. William M. Hix and Craig Moore provided constructive and insightful technical reviews of an early draft of the study.

ACRONYMS

AIT	Advanced Individual Training
ALO	Authorized Level of Organization
AMOS	Additional Military Occupational Specialty
ARNG	Army National Guard
AT	Annual Training
BCT	Basic Combat Training
DAMPL	Department of the Army Master Priority List
DMDC	Defense Manpower Data Center
DMOS	Duty military occupational specialty (assigned job)
DODOCC	Department of Defense Occupation Code
E1–E9	Enlisted paygrade levels
IADT	Initial active-duty (skill) training
MOS	Military occupational specialty
MTOE	Modified Table of Organization and Equipment
NPS	Nonprior (active-duty) service
PERSACS	Personnel Structure and Composition System
PMOS	Primary military occupational specialty (trained skill)
PS	Prior (active-duty) service
RCCPDS	Reserve Components Common Personnel Data System
SMOS	Secondary military occupational specialty
SOJT	Supervised on-the-job training
SRC	Standard Requirements Code
TOE	Table of Organization and Equipment
USAR	United States Army Reserve
YOS	Years of (reserve) service

Chapter One

INTRODUCTION

BACKGROUND

Initial training of soldiers involves two distinct phases. The first phase, called Basic Combat Training (BCT), teaches the fundamental combat skills needed by all soldiers. Subjects include rifle marksmanship, drill and ceremonies, familiarization with chemical protective equipment and so forth. The second phase, called Advanced Individual Training (AIT), instructs soldiers in the skills specific to a particular military occupational specialty (MOS). Upon graduation from this second phase, a soldier receives an alphanumeric designator that describes both the nature and level of skill. For example, the designator 11B indicates infantry skills and 13B a cannon crewman. Numerical suffixes ranging from 10 through 50 indicate skill level. Thus, the designator 13B10 would denote an entry-level cannon crewman. The award of the designator or MOS indicates the soldier is qualified in that specific skill, by which is meant that he or she has mastered some fraction of the skills associated with that military job. Soldiers are expected to round out their skills with job experience.

MOS qualification (MOSQ) is important in that it serves as a surrogate for unit readiness. A soldier not qualified in an MOS cannot deploy on a combat mission. A unit with a large number of unqualified soldiers must either replace them with qualified soldiers before it deploys or take the time to train them until they are qualified. Either course of action has a significant effect on the deployability of that unit.

Evidence suggests that average MOS qualification rates for Army Reserve (USAR) and Army National Guard (ARNG) units is 70 to 80 percent of personnel in the unit. The number of personnel in units is frequently less than the total authorized strength of a unit. A unit that has only 70 percent of its personnel MOS qualified and additional positions unfilled would require either a significant number of replacements or training prior to deployment. Experience during Operation Desert Storm in mobilizing reserve units verified that replacements and fillers were required for almost all Army component units prior to mobilization. Generally, MOS qualification poses no special problem for active component units. They normally receive MOS qualified soldiers directly from the training establishment. Soldiers who are reassigned go to similar jobs in a different unit. The situation in the reserve components is quite different.

MOSQ becomes a problem for the reserve components partly because of the nature of the personnel acquisition process. The reserves recruit a substantial number of their newcomers from those leaving the active component. These recruits, called prior-service (PS) personnel, offer some advantages in that they have the basic combat training and are qualified in an MOS. But that specific skill may or may not be one needed in the unit. If not, the unit must qualify the individual in the MOS of assignment, and that training may take a long time. Those who have never been in the military, called nonprior-service (NPS) personnel, receive both their BCT and AIT at centralized training facilities run either by the active or reserve components, but the process may take many months. In the meantime, the soldier appears on the unit rolls as not qualified in an MOS. Both PS and NPS soldiers can lower the level of MOS qualification in a unit.

Voluntary change in reassignments can exacerbate the problem. Soldiers may change units because they have relocated geographically because of civilian job changes or simple preference, and this relocation entails a change in units. Soldiers can also voluntarily change units in a local area because they can find better promotion or work opportunities in a different unit. In either case, there is no guarantee that the soldier will occupy a position requiring the same MOS as the previous unit, and the gaining unit must train the soldier in a new MOS. Again, until trained the soldier is not MOS qualified but counts against the unit strength. Depending on the MOS, re-training can take a long time.

PURPOSE

Although there are hypotheses about the general causes of low MOS qualification, we do not understand the degree to which each con-tributes to the problem. Also, it is not clear whether certain MOSs or certain types of units experience higher levels of unqualified person-nel. This report explores the causes of low skill qualification levels and whether certain skills or certain units are more difficult to main-tain at the required levels.

APPROACH AND SCOPE

The general approach taken to answer these questions involves cre-ation of a database, sampling that database, and analyzing the sam-ple with a statistical model to determine:

- What differences occur in MOSQ in specialties and units and what accounts for these differences,

- How often individuals change units or MOS and the likely driving factors behind these changes,

- How individuals changing jobs differ from those who do not, and

- How long it takes to retrain various skills.

The Database and Sample

We drew our data from three sources: the *1986 Reserve Components Surveys* (Defense Manpower Data Center, 1987) augmented with in-formation from the Defense Manpower Data Center's (DMDC's) Reserve Components Common Personnel Data System (RCCPDS) and the Army's Personnel Structure and Composition System (PERSACS). The merged database provides a comprehensive frame-work for the tracking of individual reserve skill training and turnover during FY86 and FY87. Our research concentrates on selected re-servists in the Army National Guard and the Army Reserve. Our sample is based on the 10 percent sample of enlisted reservists in these components selected for the *1986 Reserve Components Surveys.*

One aspect of the sample important for our analysis is that the survey excluded individuals attending initial active-duty training (IADT)— usually E1 or E2 personnel. Those few remaining reservists at pay grades E1 and E2 were likely to be atypical, so we restricted our analysis sample to those reservists in pay grades E3 through E9.

The initial survey provided a wealth of information not commonly available on reserve personnel files. It collected detailed individual information in seven areas: military background; military plans; military training, benefits, and programs; individual and family characteristics; civilian work; family resources; and military life. The most relevant survey information for our training analysis concerns training history and mode, civilian job characteristics, and historical information on reserve service and unit changes. Attitudinal information was also available about training, proposals for extended training time, and other aspects of reserve service. The survey records were matched with corresponding RCCPDS records to obtain information on individual unit affiliation, home and unit location, pay grade, and duty and primary occupational specialties.

Job assignments are indicated by the duty MOS (DMOS) designator on the RCCPDS tapes. The primary MOS (PMOS) indicates the primary skill in which the individual has successfully completed training. Our analysis defines a soldier as duty qualified when the PMOS and DMOS match at three character levels. Duty qualification indicates whether the soldier is assigned to a job in the primary area of training. As such, duty qualification measures how well matched assignments are relative to training and indicates whether a soldier can deploy with the unit.[1]

Earlier research (Grissmer, Buddin, and Kirby, 1989) suggested that high levels of job and unit reassignment affected skill qualification levels. The qualification rates for prior-service personnel in the FY86

---

[1]Note that the three-character match ensures training and at least minimal qualification in the correct MOS, but not necessarily at the right skill level. Thus, our analysis does not reflect the extent to which members are assigned to jobs in their MOS for which they are over- or underqualified.

survey sample did not rise rapidly with years of reserve service, which suggested that some soldiers might not remain continuously assigned in the same specialty. The qualification rates for NPS personnel actually fell with years of service (YOS), indicating possible job and unit changes for them also. The actual job assignment pattern was not available in the FY86 database, so we further augmented our database with information from the RCCPDS quarterly record for October 1987. The RCCPDS update allowed us to track changes in job assignment, unit assignment, and home location and to relate these changes to the likelihood of subsequent FY87 skill qualification.

The final set of analysis variables added to our database is unit information from the PERSACS database and aggregated unit-level data from the RCCPDS. The unit-level information is matched back with the individual soldier records from the survey. The PERSACS data provided information on mobilization priority, equipment modernization status, unit reorganizations (terminations, openings, and major requirements changes), unit type (combat, combat support, and combat service support), unit branch (infantry, armor, signal, engineering, etc.), and unit skill and grade authorizations. With the exception of the unit authorizations information, other unit characteristics were derived from the PERSACS 13-character standard requirements code (SRC) that identified the unit's Table of Organization and Equipment (TOE). Mobilization priority is based on the authorized level of organization (ALO).[2] Unit type was constructed by grouping unit branch categories into the appropriate combat, combat support, and combat service support areas. Equipment modernization status is based on the TOE series of the unit equipment and the effective date for the TOE structure change. Unit size, location, and attrition information were constructed from the RCCPDS database for the units corresponding to the soldiers in the survey sample.

_____

[2]The Department of the Army Master Priority List (DAMPL) provides a more accurate and complete characterization of the unit's mobilization priority than ALO, but ALO corresponds in general with DAMPL and has the advantage of being unclassified.

The Statistical Model

Multivariate models are used to analyze the patterns of skill qualification and personnel turnover. A three-equation recursive logit structure (Maddala, 1983; Lee, 1981; Schmidt and Strauss, 1975) is used to examine how various individual and unit characteristics affect qualification and skill reassignment. The appendix contains a more detailed discussion of the model's operation. The data allow us to determine changes in primary and duty MOS as well as unit changes and geographical migration for each reservist in the file. We can also estimate MOS qualification levels for different types of individuals and units at two points in time (June 1986 and October 1987) and determine duty reassignments during that 15-month period. We use three types of equations to explain:

- What accounts for differences in MOS qualification levels across types of individuals and units in June 1986?

- What is different about individuals changing and not changing duty MOS in the 15-month period?

- How long does retraining take across different skills?

The first equation is a snapshot of what factors affect qualification at one point in time (June 1986). This equation identifies what types of individuals are likely to be qualified or what unit characteristics are associated with high levels of individual skill qualification. The second equation examines DMOS changes between June 1986 and October 1987. The results show whether some types of individual or units are more prone to job changes and whether qualified people are more or less likely to change. The final equation examines individual qualification status (October 1987) as a function of recent assignment and job qualification as well as individual and unit characteristics. The focus of this analysis is on identifying factors that affect the requalification of individuals changing DMOS between the two periods and the qualification status of individuals who remain in their initial unit.

REPORT ORGANIZATION

The next five sections of the report are organized as follows. Chapter Two examines patterns of job training and qualification at the time of the survey in June 1986. Chapter Three describes factors associated with changing DMOS or units for the survey cohort between the time of the survey and September 1987. Chapter Four analyzes the retraining or requalification behavior of reservists changing DMOS during this 15-month interval. This chapter also examines what factors enhance the likelihood that reservists who were unqualified in their FY86 skill and did not change jobs will become qualified by September 1987. Chapters Two through Four also describe the results from the recursive logit model. In each chapter, initial description and discussion are based on simple tabulations and are followed by a detailed examination of the regression results. Summary tables in each chapter show the derivatives of the probability function for continuous variables and unit changes for indicator variables, that is, the rates of change in the estimated probabilities with changes in individual and unit characteristics. Chapter Five uses the retraining information from Chapter Four and develops estimates of skill retraining times. The final chapter provides conclusions and policy recommendations. An appendix contains a detailed discussion of the statistical model, variable definitions, and logistic regression coefficients.

Chapter Two

PATTERNS OF JOB TRAINING AND JOB QUALIFICATION

This chapter examines the 1986 data pertaining to job qualification and how it changes. It looks at, in turn, the extent to which the reserves depend on supervised on-the-job training (SOJT), the level of job qualification in units, how that level varies across units, and what variables explain this variation.

RELIANCE ON MOS EARNED IN ACTIVE-DUTY SCHOOLS

A key feature of reserve training is heavy reliance on SOJT. Although NPS personnel receive initial active-duty training (IADT) in a PMOS, Table 2.1 (taken from FY86 survey data) implies that after one year only about 80 percent have active-duty training in their current job. Part of this may be due to split training that occurs over two summers or to delays in initiating training while awaiting training school slots. However, utilization of IADT declines with YOS. Reservists remain in their IADT skill longer than guardsman, but even there about 30 percent of NPS personnel with five years of experience have no active-duty training in their PMOS.

Prior-service personnel receive a major share of their reserve training through SOJT in the local unit. Table 2.2 shows that only one-third of prior-service guardsmen and half of the reservists are initially matched with their active-duty PMOS. Thus, half or more of each group need retraining for their first reserve job assignment. The retraining burden increases with YOS as PS personnel, like NPS per-

Table 2.1

**Nonprior-Service Personnel with Active-Duty Training in Their
PMOS by Years of Reserve Service**

Years of Reserve Service	Army National Guard		Army Reserve	
	Percent	Number	Percent	Number
1	76	344	83	202
2	75	1080	82	432
3	74	1175	80	490
4	67	1116	78	407
5	64	1186	72	314
6 or more	45	5035	56	1748

Table 2.2

**Prior-Service Personnel with Active-Duty Training in Their
PMOS by Years of Reserve Service**

Years of Reserve Service	Army National Guard				Army Reserve			
	E3–E4		E5–E9		E3–E4		E5–E9	
	%	#	%	#	%	#	%	#
1	37	573	29	288	48	463	56	116
2	33	407	29	276	42	311	45	158
3	32	297	28	308	34	231	41	211
4	26	262	25	394	31	152	34	214
5	29	175	21	392	31	99	28	229
6 or more	21	514	19	4023	27	225	23	2593

sonnel, change to new jobs and need retraining. After five years of reserve service, only 20 to 30 percent of PS personnel have active-duty training in their PMOS.

In lieu of active-duty training, most receive SOJT from their reserve component. Critics of SOJT fault it for a lack of homogeneity in training methods and standards. About 15 percent of those without active-duty training in their PMOS receive some complementary OJT from their civilian jobs, but the potential for civilian transfer is limited because only 25 to 30 percent of Army reservists have civilian jobs that are even remotely related to their reserve jobs.

MOS QUALIFICATION LEVELS

Overall, USAR has lower qualification rates than the ARNG, and PS personnel have lower rates than NPS soldiers. About 17 percent of E3 to E9 personnel in the Guard were unqualified, as compared with 25 percent in the Army Reserve. Figure 2.1 shows that 12 percent and 20 percent of the NPS guardsmen and reservists, respectively, were unqualified in their assigned jobs. For PS personnel, 23 percent of the guardsmen and 29 percent of the reservists were unqualified.

Qualification levels can vary by type of unit or type of skill. More personnel are unqualified in combat service support units (20 percent) in the Guard than either combat (15 percent) or combat support (16 percent) units (see Figure 2.2). However, the percentage not qualified is approximately equal for different types of units in the Army Reserve. Individuals in combat skills have a significantly lower probability of being not qualified than those in noncombat skills (see Figure 2.3). Only 8 percent of combat skills are not qualified in the Guard compared with 25 percent for high-skilled noncombat jobs and 20 percent for low-skilled noncombat jobs. A similar but less pronounced pattern occurs in the Army Reserve.

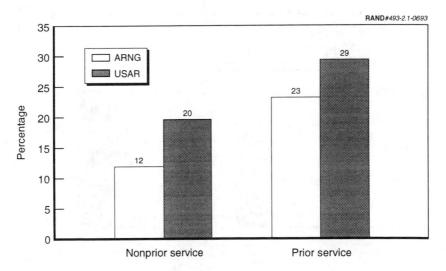

Figure 2.1—Percentage of E3–E9 Reservists Not Skill Qualified

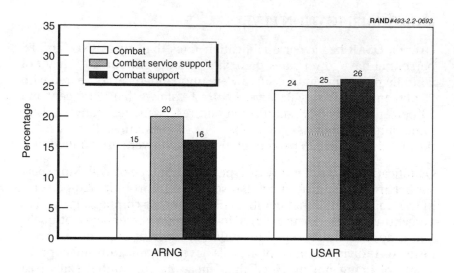

Figure 2.2—Percentage of E3–E9 Personnel Not Qualified in Different Types of Units

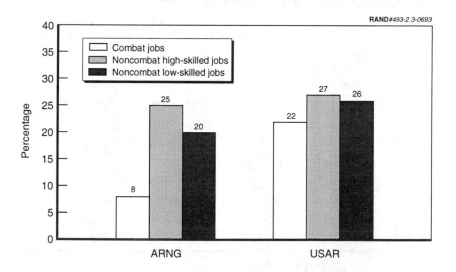

Figure 2.3—Percentage of E3–E9 Reservists with Different Skills Not Qualified

One explanation of the difference in qualification levels between the Guard and Reserve is that the Guard has more combat units, which tend to have higher qualification levels. Qualification levels of non-combat personnel in the Guard and Reserve are somewhat similar. High-skilled noncombat jobs have 25 and 27 percent not qualified in the Guard and Reserve, respectively, whereas low-skilled noncombat jobs have 20 and 26 percent not qualified. Combat jobs might have lower levels not qualified because individuals stay in those jobs longer.

We also examined data on two other areas that might explain differences in qualification levels: modernization and mobilization. When units modernize their equipment, personnel must be re-trained on the new equipment. Consequently, we expected lower qualification levels in Guard units with the newest equipment (Series J). Units with Series J equipment had qualification rates of 78 percent in contrast to 84 percent for other units. About 15 percent of Guard units were Series J units. The relatively small difference in qualification rates for such units could indicate rapid retraining rates or that the designation might not be given until retraining is accomplished. In the Army Reserve, only 2 percent of units were Series J, and they had no difference in qualification from other units.

Units may be filled to different levels of equipment and personnel depending upon their priority for mobilization. This characteristic is called the Authorized Level of Organization (ALO), and the particular level a unit is permitted is signified by a numerical suffix (1–4).[1] We find that ALO-1 units have somewhat higher levels of unqualified personnel than ALO-2 or -3 units (see Figure 2.4). About 20 percent of guardsmen in ALO-1 units were unqualified as compared with about 15 percent of guardsmen in ALO-2 and -3 units. In the Army Reserve, a similar pattern emerges: 26 percent of ALO-1 personnel are not qualified compared with 23 percent of ALO-2 and ALO-3.

---

[1]ALO-1 units are authorized at 100 percent of the modified TOE (MTOE), as compared with 90 and 80 percent of MTOE for ALO-2 and ALO-3 units, respectively. MTOE reflects the wartime requirements of the unit.

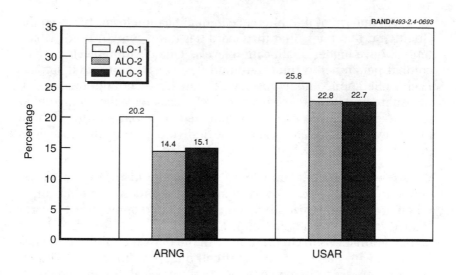

Figure 2.4—Percentage of Reservists Not Qualified by ALO

One possible explanation for the lower qualification of ALO-1 units is that they are predominantly combat support and service support units. Earlier we saw that these units have lower qualification levels than combat units. Our statistical model allows us to determine whether the additional resources enjoyed by ALO-1 units raise qualification levels, after other characteristics of the unit and personnel in the unit are considered. The next section provides regression results estimated on June 1986 qualification levels. These results demonstrate the influence of the various factors while controlling for others.

LOGISTIC MODEL OF DUTY QUALIFICATION IN FY86

The remainder of this chapter uses a multivariate model to describe how duty qualification levels in FY86 vary with individual and unit characteristics. The multivariate model estimates the relationship between individual skill qualification and soldier's experience, pay grade, education/aptitude, job skill, unit reassignment, unit size and attrition, unit equipment modernization, and unit type. Four model specifications are estimated, distinguishing NPS and PS personnel for the ARNG and USAR.

The FY86 qualification equation provides a snapshot picture of what type of individuals are most likely to be qualified at a point in time and whether individual qualification rates are higher in some types of units than others. This section is based on cross-sectional evidence from the *1986 Surveys* and merged information on unit characteristics. The equation is the first piece of the broader, three-equation model described earlier that examines the dynamics of job qualification, job turbulence or reassignment, and subsequent requalification in a new skill.

Soldier Characteristics and Skill Qualification in FY86

We first consider the relationship between YOS and qualification rate. We had hypothesized that prior- and nonprior-service personnel would have different patterns of qualification as they entered and stayed in the force. The relationship between duty qualification and YOS early in the career provides an indication of the quasi-learning curve for reservists. We say "quasi-learning curve" because a true learning curve would reflect how quickly reservists would become qualified if they were continuously assigned in a given skill. However, the database does not provide an indication of continuous assignment, so the observed relationship is a quasi-learning curve that indicates how many become qualified over time net of retraining and reassignments within the unit.

Holding constant other soldier and unit characteristics, Table 2.3 shows how we would expect the qualification rate for nonprior- and prior-service personnel to change with YOS. For the moment, we have assumed that individuals do not change units—defined as moving between battalion-sized units—but can be reassigned within the unit.

For NPS personnel, the effects of intraunit reassignment dominate those of learning, so the net qualification rate falls. In effect, individuals tend to switch to new jobs within the unit at sufficient rates to offset any reduction in qualification associated with individual members becoming qualified at their current jobs. The qualification levels of Guard personnel remain above those for Reserve personnel.

Table 2.3

**Predicted Duty Qualification Percentage
by Years of Reserve Service
(assumes no unit change)**

Years of Reserve Service	Army National Guard		Army Reserve	
	NPS	PS	NPS	PS
1	93.4	70.8	86.7	64.3
2	93.0	73.4	86.2	67.6
3	92.6	75.6	85.7	70.5
4	92.2	77.5	85.3	73.0
5	91.8	79.2	84.9	75.1
6	91.3	80.7	84.5	76.9
7	90.9	81.9	84.1	78.4
8	90.5	83.0	83.8	79.5
9	90.0	83.8	83.5	80.5
10	89.6	84.6	83.2	81.2

PS personnel also have higher qualification rates in the Guard than in the Army Reserve. The Guard has a much lower match (see Table 2.2) between active-duty and reserve jobs than the Reserve, but apparently the Guard is more successful in quickly retraining unmatched personnel than the Reserve. Table 2.3 shows that the qualification rates of PS personnel rise slowly with YOS in both components, with 20 to 25 percent of personnel unqualified at the five-year mark. As with NPS personnel, the PS learning curves are probably biased by intraunit reassignment, that is, a group of individuals assigned to the same skill within a unit would probably become qualified at a job more quickly than is reflected in Table 2.3. Nonetheless, the evidence shows that qualification is not simply a problem for new recruits entering the reserves, but rather a persistent and even greater problem for PS personnel throughout their reserve careers.

Unit changes exacerbate reserve qualification problems. Table 2.4 shows that 40 to 50 percent of Army reservists have changed units at least once. The probability of unit change tends to rise with years of reserve service and is higher for PS than for NPS personnel. Frequently, the new unit will not have job openings available in the reservist's previous skill, so job reassignment and retraining will be necessary.

Table 2.4

Percentage of Reservists Who Have Served in More than One Unit by Years of Reserve Service

Years of Reserve Service	Army National Guard		Army Reserve	
	NPS	PS	NPS	PS
1 or less	4	13	9	12
2	16	27	16	22
3	24	36	24	36
4	29	50	33	39
5	39	49	40	49
6	33	54	43	45
7	41	61	53	56
8	44	59	48	52
9	34	56	58	69
10 or more	59	67	75	77
Overall	39	48	47	49

Table 2.5 illustrates the adverse effect of unit change on individual job qualification. Other things equal, the immediate effect of a unit change is a 25 to 30 percentage point reduction in the probability that the individual soldier will be qualified. The recovery period for the qualification rate is several years. Five years after the change, the qualification rate for PS personnel has just matched that before the change, whereas the NPS qualification rate is still several percentage points below the prechange rate. Skill switching in the new unit and protracted retraining time in SOJT programs extend the recovery period.

Tables 2.6 and 2.7 show the effect of other individual and unit characteristics on job qualification. One could assume that such unit traits as modernization of equipment or higher mobilization status might have some effect on the level of job qualification. On the individual level, one might assume that individual aptitude or education level might also affect qualification. Table 2.6 examines pay grade, education and aptitude, and job areas. It shows that qualification rates do not differ much by pay grade. For the most part, E4 to E9 personnel are more likely to be skill qualified than E3 personnel. However, there is little difference in skill qualification by grade for

Table 2.5

Unit Change and Predicted Duty Qualification Percentage by Years of Reserve Service (assumes unit change at 3 YOS)

Years of Reserve Service	Army National Guard		Army Reserve	
	NPS	PS	NPS	PS
1	93	71	87	64
2	93	73	86	68
Before unit change	93	76	86	70
After unit change	61	50	52	43
4	66	57	58	49
5	71	64	63	55
6	76	70	68	61
7	79	75	73	66
8	83	79	77	70
9	86	83	81	74
10	89	86	84	77

Table 2.6

Differences in FY86 Duty Qualification Percentages by Individual Characteristics

Characteristic	Army National Guard		Army Reserve	
	NPS	PS	NPS	PS
Change unit	−30.35**	−21.01**	−30.88**	−24.33**
Pay grade				
E4	1.83	4.19	2.72	12.71**
E5	3.85**	7.88*	5.41*	17.72**
E6	3.34*	8.46*	5.73	18.36**
E7	3.71	9.17**	0.87	16.64**
E8	5.18*	8.98*	1.91	7.22
E9	−6.55	12.70	−10.79	20.49**
Education/aptitude				
Nongraduate	−0.31	1.00	0.78	−0.77
Education > 12	−1.15	−2.78*	−1.67	−1.71
AFQT Cat. III	−0.25	0.91	4.03*	5.93**
AFQT Cat. IV, V	1.23	4.56	1.09	9.18**
Job area				
High skill	−24.24**	−25.99**	−10.47**	−6.23*
Low skill	−14.05**	−14.06**	−9.10**	−3.80

NOTE: The reference categories are no unit change, E3, high school graduate, AFQT Category I or II, and combat skill. Starred and double-starred entries are based on logistic regression coefficients that differ significantly from zero at the 5 and 1 percent confidence levels, respectively.

Table 2.7

**Differences in FY86 Duty Qualification Percentages
by Unit Characteristics**

Characteristic	Army National Guard		Army Reserve	
	NPS	PS	NPS	PS
Unit size				
51–100	−0.36	−6.50**	−2.32	−4.16
101–150	0.09	−5.49*	−1.04	−0.20
151–200	1.78	−6.14**	1.15	−1.25
201 or more	2.02	−5.57	0.29	0.32
Unit attrition (%)				
YOS 1 – 4	−0.01	−0.03	−0.08*	−0.03
YOS 5 – 9	0.01	0.00	0.00	−0.00
YOS 10 – 19	0.00	−0.04	−0.10	−0.13*
YOS 20 or more	−0.00	−0.02	0.00	−0.01
Series J TOE	−8.45**	−4.37*	−8.01	3.75
mobilization status				
ALO-1	−1.59	−6.71*	4.43	0.07
ALO-2	−1.22	−3.25	3.46	5.65
ALO-3	−2.19	−6.91*	5.32	−0.54
Unit type				
Combat	−5.21**	−1.54	−4.02	−4.80
Combat support	−2.30	1.22	−3.16	−6.39**

NOTE: The reference categories are unit size 1 to 50, TOE series other than J, ALO level lower than 3, and combat service support unit. Starred and double-starred entries are based on logistic regression coefficients that differ significantly from zero at the 5 and 1 percent confidence levels, respectively.

those between E4 and E9. Furthermore, an individual recruit's education or aptitude also apparently has little to do with his or her qualification rates. High school graduates do not have qualification rates significantly different from those of nongraduates or those with some schooling beyond high school. Scores on the Armed Forces Qualification Test (AFQT) have no effect on the qualification rate of NPS or PS guardsmen. USAR personnel are *more* likely to be skill qualified if they are in lower AFQT aptitude groups.

The final group of individual characteristics is the job area, and this characteristic appears to make a difference in job qualification. We defined three job areas for our analysis: combat jobs, high-skilled noncombat jobs, and low-skilled noncombat jobs.[2] Generally, noncombat jobs have lower qualification rates than combat, and within the noncombat jobs, the higher the skills required, the lower the qualification. In the Guard, the qualification rates were 25 and 14 percentage points lower in the high- and low-skilled noncombat jobs than in the combat jobs. Skill differences in qualification rates follow the same general pattern in the Army Reserve as in the Guard, but the differences are much smaller. Qualification rates are 10 and 6 percentage points lower for USAR NPS and PS personnel in high-skilled noncombat jobs, respectively, as those in combat jobs.

Unit Characteristics and Skill Qualification in FY86

Turning to unit characteristics, we find, other things equal, that they have small and typically statistically insignificant effects on the probability of individual skill qualification. High levels of unit attrition might lead to job shortages and reassignment, so unit attrition and qualification were expected to be inversely related. In fact, qualification rates do not vary significantly with unit attrition. Nor does unit size have much effect on qualification. The qualification rates of PS guardsmen are about 6 percentage points lower if they are in units larger than 50 than in the smallest size units. Equipment modernization reduced the qualification rates of NPS and PS personnel by about 8 and 4 percentage points, but the difference is statistically significant only in the Guard.

Controlling for other factors, the mobilization status of the reservist's unit has little effect on his or her probability of being skill qualified. Guard and Reserve units are unable to achieve higher qualification rates in higher priority units. Although higher priority units are resourced at higher levels, they have the same difficulties in achieving and maintaining skill qualified personnel as other units.

---

[2]This classification is based on one-digit DoD occupation codes (DODOCC). Combat jobs are defined as DODOCC 0: infantry, gun crews, and seamanship specialists. High-skilled noncombat jobs are defined as DODOCC 1–4: electronic equipment repairmen, communications and intelligence specialists, medical and dental specialists, and other technical and allied specialists. Low-skilled noncombat jobs are defined as DODOCC 5–8: functional support and administration, electrical/mechanical equipment repairmen, craftsmen, and service and supply handlers.

Qualification rates do not differ much among combat, combat support, and combat service support units. For NPS ARNG, rates are 5 percentage points lower in combat units than in combat service support units. Other things equal, PS reservists in combat support units have qualification rates about 6 percentage points lower than those in other types of units. The modest and generally insignificant effects of unit type on qualification contrast sharply with the effects of individual job area on qualification levels.

SUMMARY AND UNRESOLVED ISSUES FROM ANALYSIS OF FY86 SKILL QUALIFICATION

A number of important generalizations emerge from our analysis of the 1986 data.

- **Army Guard and Reserve personnel rely markedly on skills learned outside the active Army school system.**

Only some 50 percent of nonprior-service personnel are still using their IADT preparation after six years. Whereas approximately one-third to one-half of prior-service personnel at entry into the reserves use active skills, only about 20–25 percent of prior-service personnel use those skills after six years in the reserves. The reserves retrain individuals extensively and depend on SOJT, local reserve schools and Guard academies, and civilian-acquired skills as a basis for retraining.

- **Between 16 and 25 percent of the reservists are not qualified in their jobs.**

MOS qualification rates for E3 to E9 in June 1986 was 84 percent in the Guard and 75 percent in the Army Reserve. Qualification rates were higher for nonprior-service personnel (88 percent in the Guard and 80 percent in the Reserve) than for prior-service personnel (77 percent in the Guard and 71 percent in the Reserve).

- **Two factors have the largest effect on job qualification: individuals changing units and the type of job held.**

Individuals changing units are a main cause of lowered MOS qualification rates. Individuals who change units have qualification rates

25–30 percentage points below those not changing units, and unit changers are likely to remain unqualified for several years. We will explore the causes of these unit changes more extensively in the next chapter. The second most important factor in determining qualification rate is the type of job. In the Guard, combat jobs had qualification rates 14 and 24 percentage points higher than low- and high-skilled noncombat jobs, respectively. Other things equal, NPS reservists in combat jobs have qualification rates about 10 percent higher than noncombat jobs, whereas PS reservists in high-skill jobs had qualification rates 6 percent below those of combat jobs.

- **Other individual and unit characteristics did not significantly affect qualification rates.**

Qualification rates varied little by individuals' education or AFQT score and only slightly more with pay grade. Although E3 personnel had lower qualification rates, individuals in pay grades E4 through E9 had nearly equal chances of being qualified. Nor did qualification rates depend critically on unit characteristics. Units with Series J TOE in the Guard had somewhat lower qualification (78 percent) rates than other units (84 percent), and this difference remains after controlling for other unit characteristics and composition. Units with higher mobilization priority did not have higher qualification rates than other units. After controlling for job type and other factors, little difference remained among combat, combat support, and combat service support units in their qualification rates.

WHAT THE FY86 ANALYSIS DID NOT REVEAL

The FY86 analysis shows that skill reassignment and retraining have a substantial effect on individual skill qualification, but the snapshot picture does not provide evidence on the extent of reassignment. Similarly, job reassignment has limited the usefulness of the FY86 data in inferring how long it takes reservists to become skill qualified in a new job if the reservist remains continuously assigned to a job. The follow-up data allow us to track assignment changes between FY86 and FY87 and to measure how long it takes reassigned soldiers to become requalified in their new skills.

Whereas unit change is a major factor in low qualification rates, the FY86 data provide no evidence on why unit change is so common. If the primary reason for unit changes was relocation of reservists for new civilian jobs, then the cost of unit change turbulence would be inherent in reserve reliance on hiring part-time workers in the local labor market. Alternatively, if reservists changed units for better promotion opportunities, then the reserves could consider policies to reduce incentives for reserve units to compete with each other for personnel.

Chapter Three

CHANGING JOBS AND CHANGING UNITS

Either the unit commander or the individual in the reserve components can initiate a job change. As vacancies occur in reserve positions, the unit commander may choose to fill them from new prior- or nonprior-service recruits or from reassignment within the unit. The individual can also seek better assignments, promotion, and more pay through job searches in different units or components. In this chapter, we will explore the frequency of job changes and the relationship between job changes and unit transfers. We consider job changes over the 15-month period from June 1986 through September 1987 for E3 to E9 personnel. We begin with an examination of general patterns of job and unit change before turning to a multivariate model of job change that controls for individual and unit characteristics as well as unit change.

CHANGING JOBS

The patterns of job change are relatively complex and the effects are not immediately clear. Job changes occur within units, between like and different units, and within and between components. Whatever the pattern and reasons, a significant number of reservists change jobs. More people who are not qualified in their present duty change jobs than those who are qualified, but even among this latter group switching is common. Switching that occurs before qualification for the current job could indicate an inability to qualify for the current job or switching into a job for which an individual is qualified. For instance, a prior-service accession may join in a job for which he/she is not qualified, but switch if a job opening occurs in which he/she is qualified. So job switching may in some cases be useful.

Figure 3.1 shows that approximately 21 percent of ARNG and 32 percent of USAR personnel in our sample changed DMOS in the 15-month period. DMOS change was slightly more prevalent among prior-service personnel in the Guard, but not in the Reserve. The proportion of personnel changing jobs was significantly higher among those who were not duty qualified in 1986 than among those who were (see Figure 3.2).

The unqualified personnel in June 1986 presumably were in training for a DMOS, but 37 percent of these guardsmen and 47 percent of the reservists switched to another DMOS by September 1987. This switching may have occurred because better job matches were found for recent prior-service personnel, because individuals could not learn the original jobs, or because they did not like those jobs. Job switching may be efficient or inefficient, depending on the cause.

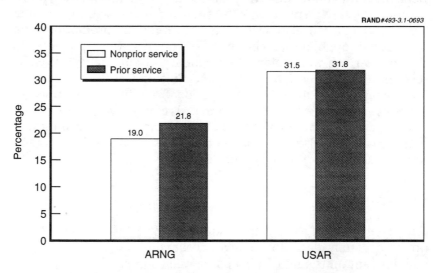

Figure 3.1—Percentage of Army Guard and Army Reserve in Sample Changing DMOS

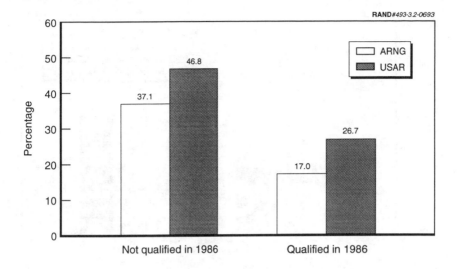

Figure 3.2—Percentage Changing DMOS by Qualification Status
in June 1986

Among those already duty qualified in the Guard, switching was much more common from noncombat high-skilled jobs (see Figure 3.3). Only 14.4 percent of individuals switched from combat jobs in the period, whereas 36 percent switched from noncombat skilled jobs. For the Army Reserve, there were scant differences among combat and noncombat skills in percentage switching DMOS. Approximately 25 percent of qualified individuals from all skills changed jobs. Switching from noncombat skilled jobs may be particularly inefficient since the investment in previous training is higher and retraining individuals into these positions takes longer. From this viewpoint, barriers to switching should be higher for noncombat skilled jobs. But in fact, individuals who were not qualified in their DMOS in 1986 changed to another DMOS more often if they were training in high-skilled noncombat skills than in combat jobs (see Figure 3.4).

For the Guard, the net effect of job switching is to leave the occupation distribution about the same as before switching (see Figure 3.5). The figure shows that there is about the same flow of individuals to

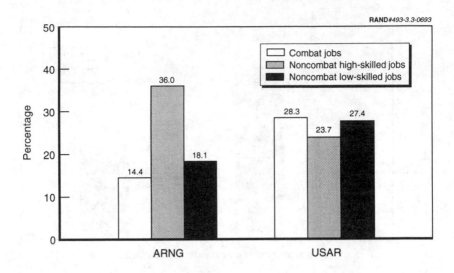

Figure 3.3—Percentage Switching Jobs by Type of Job for the
Qualified Group

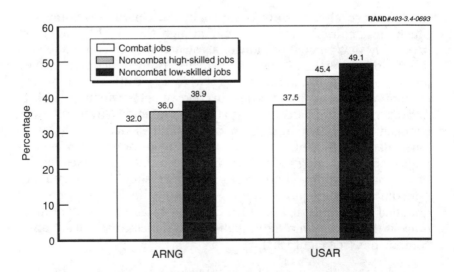

Figure 3.4—Percentage Switching Jobs by Type of Job for the
Unqualified Group

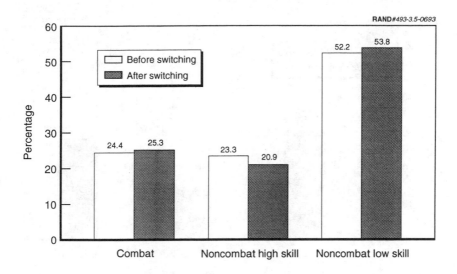

Figure 3.5—Net Effect of Job Switching: ARNG

each of the job groups as away from each. However, for the Army Reserve (see Figure 3.6), individuals prefer retraining in combat jobs at the expense of low-skilled noncombat jobs.

We have classified individuals who switch units into three groups: those changing units within a component, those changing to another Army component, and those changing to another service's component. For the Guard, only 70.4 percent of individuals were in the same unit after 15 months. Those changing units within the Guard constituted 15.4 percent, whereas 11 percent of the sample left the Selected Reserve, 2.7 percent joined the Army Reserve, and .5 percent joined the reserves of another service. For the Reserve, 69.6 percent were in the same unit after 15 months. Attrition was 7.8 percent, and 1.7 percent joined the Guard, .5 percent joined a non-Army component, and 20.3 percent changed units internally.

Figure 3.7 shows the percentage of each of these groups that changed DMOS. Those who changed components were the most likely to switch jobs. Over 90 percent of the members of the ARNG who go to the USAR require training. This high percentage probably reflects

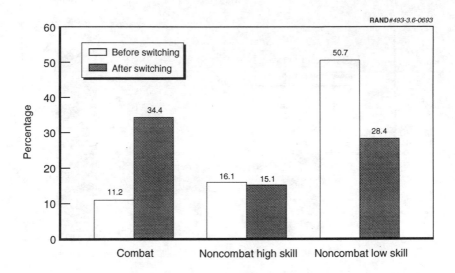

Figure 3.6—Net Effect of Job Switching: USAR

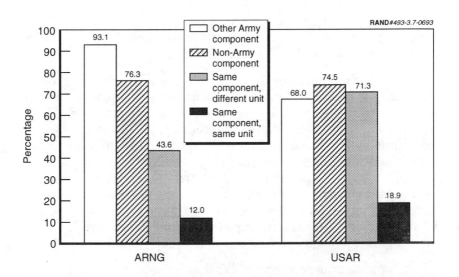

Figure 3.7—Percentage Changing DMOS Among Different Groups

the fact that the Guard is heavy in combat jobs and the Army Reserve has few combat jobs. Switching DMOS was also quite prevalent among those switching units within the same component. For the Guard, 44 percent of internal unit switchers also changed jobs, as did 71 percent in the Reserve. Individuals who remained in the same unit changed DMOS at significantly lower rates—12 percent for the Guard and 19 percent for the Reserve, but even these rates require substantial amounts of unit time and resources for retraining.

Interunit transfers account for a significant share of retraining requirements for each component. Figure 3.8 shows those present in June 1986 requiring retraining during the 15-month period from our sample. In the Guard, about 46 percent (100 + 1210/2827) of retraining requirements arise from individuals transferring units, whereas for the Reserve, 60 percent (100 + 1256/2842) of the retraining required is for transfers from other units.

These interunit transfers can result in a significant share of individuals not being qualified in September 1987. Figure 3.9 shows the proportion of individuals in each group who are retrained at the end of the period. For the Guard, those individuals coming from the

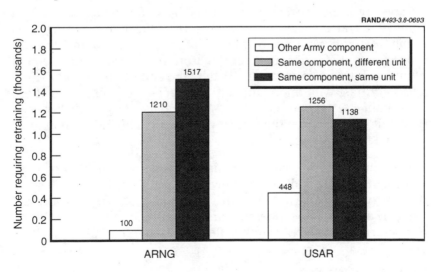

Figure 3.8—Sources of Retraining Requirements from Our Sample

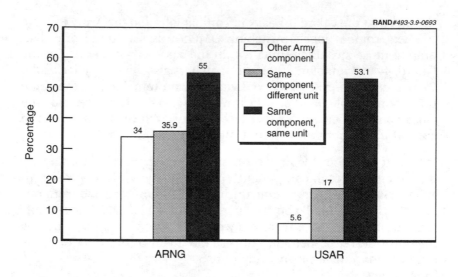

Figure 3.9—Percentage of Those Changing DMOS Between June 1986
and September 1987 Who Are Retrained by September 1987

Reserve and those transferring units have the lowest retraining completion rates. Only about 35 percent of those transferring units in the Guard are retrained by the end of the period. For the Reserve, only 6 percent of individuals coming from the Guard and 17 percent of interunit transfers are requalified by the end of the period. These levels contrast with approximately 55 percent requalified for those who change DMOS but not units. Individuals transferring between units not only generate the largest training load but also remain unqualified for longer periods.

Some individuals may change components in order to change jobs. Significantly more individuals flow from the Guard to the Reserve than from the Reserve to the Guard. In the 15-month period, 481 (2.7 percent) of Guard personnel transferred to the Reserve, but only 147 (1.7 percent) transferred from the Reserve to the Guard.

CHANGING UNITS

Evidence on the frequency of unit change shows patterns similar to that of job change. Reservists were asked on the 1986 survey of reserve forces how long they had been in the reserves and how long they had been in their present unit. Table 2.4 shows—as should be expected—that the longer individuals stay in the reserves, the more likely they are to have changed units. Prior-service personnel change units most frequently, and the gap between PS and NPS personnel is much larger in the ARNG than in the USAR. NPS personnel in the USAR have higher unit change levels than do NPS personnel in the ARNG.

Three explanations are possible for the higher unit transfer rates of prior-service personnel. Prior-service personnel may be preferred for promotion and higher ranking positions that accompany unit changes. Second, prior-service personnel are older and have more military experience at similar years of reserve service, so they may be more adept at internal job search and finding new positions. They also have more to gain from promotion because longer military service entitles them to higher retirement annuities. Third, prior-service personnel may migrate more frequently than nonprior-service personnel because of civilian job opportunities. These moves would be accompanied by unit changes.

A way of determining unit change frequency for reservists is to follow a sample of reservists longitudinally and check unit status at two points in time. Table 3.1 shows that 20.8 percent of guardsmen and 24.4 percent of reservists changed units between June 1986 and September 1987. Prior-service personnel had somewhat higher transfer rates than nonprior-service personnel, and reservists had slightly higher transfer rates than guardsmen.

Table 3.1

**Percentage Changing Units Between
June 1986 and September 1987**

Army National Guard	
NPS	19.8
PS	22.1
Overall	20.8
Army Reserve	
NPS	23.8
PS	24.8
Overall	24.4

Table 3.2 shows that lower (E3 and E4) and higher (E7 to E9) grade reservists tend to change units more frequently than those in middle grades. It also shows that most individuals changing units change battalions rather than join other units in the same battalion. For the Army Reserve, almost all unit transfers are between battalions. For the Guard, about one-third of unit transfers are to companies in the same battalion. This difference simply reflects the different organizational structure of the Guard, which has more companies organized into battalions. Companies of Guard battalions usually are located in the same or neighboring towns or cities.

The most interesting question emerging from the various reasons for changing units is whether unit transfers are motivated by civilian job considerations or by voluntary switching between local units. Table 3.3 provides a picture of the local market for Army Reserve units. It shows that reservists have a wide choice of units. Ninety percent of reservists and 84 percent of guardsmen have more than ten units within 50 miles of their homes. Less than 2 percent of guardsmen and reservists have fewer than three units within 50 miles of home. Guardsmen have somewhat less choice than reservists because Army

Table 3.2

**Percentage of Reservists Changing Units Between
June 1986 and September 1987
(by component, prior service, and pay grade)**

	E3–E4		E5–E6		E7–E9	
	NPS	PS	NPS	PS	NPS	PS
Army National Guard						
unit change	18.4	22.1	18.3	19.8	20.1	22.5
Intrabattalion	5.7	6.7	6.7	6.0	7.8	8.0
Interbattalion	12.7	15.4	11.6	13.8	12.3	14.5
Army Reserve						
unit change	24.4	25.6	21.1	21.4	26.1	29.8
Intrabattalion	1.4	1.7	2.7	2.9	4.1	6.1
Interbattalion	23.0	23.9	18.4	18.5	22.0	23.7

Table 3.3

Reservists' Choice of Units Within Given Distance from Home

	Miles	Percentage of Reservists Having Choice of				
		No Units	One Unit	2–5 Units	6–10 Units	More Than 10 Units
Army National Guard						
	25	2.5	8.3	28.9	18.4	41.8
	50	.4	1.4	13.8	7.2	83.8
	100	.0	.1	2.6	2.0	96.0
Army Reserve						
	25	1.5	4.0	21.0	13.8	59.6
	50	.1	.4	3.4	6.7	89.5
	100	.0	.0	.4	.8	98.8

Reserve units are more often located in larger cities. However, the data clearly show the possibility of an active internal labor market with considerable opportunity to search for positions among many units.

Given that reservists have considerable choice among units, the next step is to determine how far apart are the units involved in unit transfer. Figure 3.10 shows that two-thirds of unit transfers are between units located less than five miles apart. Only 20 percent of unit transfers are between units located greater than 50 miles apart. These data reinforce the perception that there are active internal local reserve labor markets within which individuals either voluntarily switch or are reassigned. Since most transfers are between battalions, it is unlikely that many reservists are reassigned as a result of transfers directed by the unit or component. A large number of transfers within battalions might suggest reassignments directed to balance strengths or to fill critical vacancies. Reassignments between battalions suggest that voluntary transfers are the likely source of most unit transfers.

Reservists have several incentives to transfer units voluntarily—increased opportunity for promotion, "better" job assignment, or a job-compatible civilian schedule. There appears to be little review of unit transfers within components to determine if they are in the best

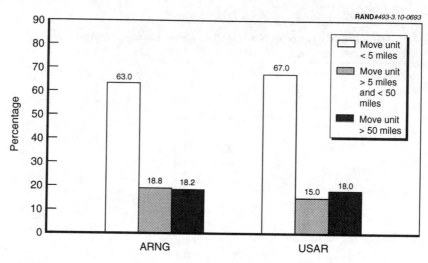

Figure 3.10—Percentage of Unit Changes by Distance Between Units

interest of the component. Transfers may enhance reserve readiness if the promotion and transfer processes fill vacancies with individuals already trained or who can quickly and efficiently learn new job skills. However, transfers that require retraining will obviously cost more than those requiring no retraining. They will be especially costly if individuals have not served in their pretransfer DMOS for long periods before transfer and retraining.

Figure 3.11 shows a strong pattern for the Guard of enhanced promotion opportunity for those who switch units. Between 27 and 32 percent of individuals switching units were promoted, compared with 22.7 percent for those not switching units. For the Army Reserve, there appears to be no relationship between promotion and unit switching. Promotion opportunity is actually decreased for those switching units locally, and is about the same for more distant moves. This may indicate a fundamentally different motivation for unit switching in the Guard and Reserve. For the Guard, promotion opportunity may be dominant, whereas for the Reserve, changing jobs may be more important.

Table 3.4 shows how frequently reservists who change units also change jobs. Only 62 percent of E3 to E9 guardsmen and 56 percent

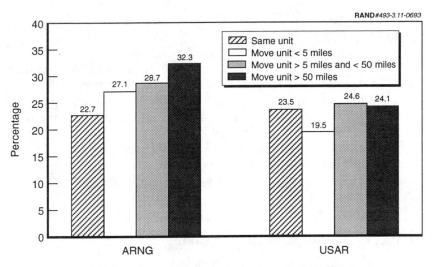

Figure 3.11—Promotion Opportunity and Unit Change

Table 3.4

**Job Turbulence and Unit Transfer Patterns Between
June 1986 and September 1987
(movement over 15 months)**

	Percent of Reservists	
	ARNG	USAR
Same job, same unit	62	56
Same job, different unit	9	7
Different job, same unit	8	13
Different job, different unit	10	16
Left reserve components	11	8
	100	100

of reservists had the same job and same unit after 15 months. Some 19 percent of guardsmen and 23 percent of reservists changed units by September 1987. Of those who changed units, slightly less than half of the Guardsmen and about 70 percent of the Reservists also changed DMOS. The Guard/Reserve differences probably represent the fact that more Guard transfers are within-battalion transfers where similar jobs may be available.

LOGISTIC MODEL OF JOB CHANGE BETWEEN FY86 AND FY87

A multivariate recursive logit model was used to estimate how individual job change behavior depends on soldier experience, pay grade, education/aptitude, job area, residence/unit change, FY86 qualification status, unit size and attrition, unit equipment modernization, and unit type. The model allows us to sort out the relationship between job reassignment and other factors after controlling for the probability of unit change. Again, four model specifications are estimated, distinguishing NPS and PS personnel for the ARNG and USAR.

Soldier Characteristics and Job Change

Table 3.5 reiterates the point that unit change and job change are closely related.

Other factors constant, about 80 percent of the guardsmen who changed units also changed DMOS, contrasted with just 15 percent for those who did not change units. Among Army reservists, DMOS change is nearly coincident with unit change for those changing to a unit within five miles of their original unit: over 90 percent of these unit changes also involved changing DMOS. DMOS change is not quite as closely tied with unit change for units more than five miles from the original unit, but the probability of a DMOS change is still about 50 percentage points higher than if the member stayed in the original unit. In each component, unit change has a similar effect on DMOS change for both nonprior- and prior-service personnel.

Some reservists must change units because they have moved away from their initial units for reasons unrelated to their reserve participation (e.g., they change civilian jobs). In these circumstances, it would be harder to find a suitable job match, so residence changes are likely to increase the probability of DMOS change over and above their effect through unit change. Residence change does generally increase the probability of DMOS change by 5 to 10 percentage points, although many types of residence moves apparently have no statistically significant effect on DMOS change.

Table 3.5

Differences in DMOS Change Percentages During 15-Month Interval by Individual Characteristics

Characteristic	Army National Guard		Army Reserve	
	NPS	PS	NPS	PS
Prior unit change	3.92*	3.21	1.99	1.53
Pay grade				
E4	–0.15	0.48	8.07*	1.81
E5	4.56*	0.72	18.68**	–0.36
E6	10.30**	–0.60	18.85**	3.53
E7	19.32**	10.58	29.80**	12.24
E8	74.88**	50.17**	57.97**	44.41**
E9	–1.64	–1.12	–0.47	–3.33
Education/aptitude				
Nongraduate	3.33**	0.20	3.72	2.15
Education > 12	6.17**	2.24	4.08	0.80
AFQT Cat III	–1.49	–2.52	–3.97	–1.76
AFQT Cat IV, V	–4.55*	–3.16	–5.04	–4.53
Job area				
High skill	4.78**	8.10**	–11.31**	3.56
Low skill	7.82**	4.83**	1.09	11.09**
Changed residence				
0 to 5 miles	2.75	7.49**	7.12*	3.09
6 to 50 miles	4.57*	0.88	–1.99	–0.77
> 50 miles	7.09**	7.21	3.00	9.97*
Changed unit				
0 to 5 miles	66.12**	63.20**	73.82**	70.40**
6 to 50 miles	67.15**	62.27**	57.04**	57.51**
> 50 miles	63.25**	65.55**	49.72**	53.38**
Qualified 1986	–21.42**	–23.51**	–20.10**	–18.31**

NOTE: The reference categories are no prior unit change, E3, high school graduate, AFQT Category I or II, combat skill, no residence change, no unit change, and not duty qualified in FY86. Starred and double-starred entries are based on logistic regression coefficients that differ significantly from zero at the 5 and 1 percent confidence levels, respectively.

Table 3.5 also indicates that qualified soldiers are less likely to be change DMOS than unqualified soldiers. In general, a larger training investment is lost by reassigning a qualified soldier than a soldier who has not yet completed training in an assigned job. After controlling for other factors, reservists who were qualified in FY86 have DMOS change rates about 20 percentage points lower than those who were not qualified in FY86. This difference is more than twice the unconditional gap described in Figure 3.2, and may occur either because individuals are failing to qualify or because an opening occurs for which they are qualified.

The frequency of DMOS change increases with pay grade for non-prior-service personnel in both the Guard and Reserve, because cross-training is required as part of career progression. Surprisingly, DMOS change does not vary significantly with pay grade for prior-service personnel, although E8 personnel are much more likely to change DMOS than other prior-service personnel.

DMOS change does not vary much with either education level or aptitude. The only significant differences are for nonprior-service guardsmen: high school graduates are 3 and 6 percentage points less likely than nongraduates and those with post-high school training to change DMOS, and guardsmen in AFQT Categories IV and V have DMOS change rates about 5 percentage points lower than those in Categories I and II.

DMOS change rates also vary significantly with individual job skill. In the Guard, soldiers in low-skilled or high-skilled noncombat jobs have DMOS change rates 5 to 8 percentage points higher than those in combat skills. Among guardsmen in noncombat skills, high-skilled jobs have greater turbulence than low-skilled jobs for prior-service personnel, and the pattern is reversed for nonprior-service personnel. In the USAR, nonprior-service personnel in combat and low-skilled noncombat jobs have similar DMOS change rates that are about 11 percentage points higher than those in high-skilled non-combat jobs. For prior-service personnel in the Army Reserve, DMOS turbulence is largest in low-skilled noncombat jobs.

After controlling for other factors like unit change and qualification status, we expected that DMOS change would tend to decline with years of reserve experience because soldiers would settle into jobs for which they were well-suited. Table 3.6 shows that DMOS change does decline with years of experience, but that even reservists continuously assigned to a single unit are likely to require frequent retraining. About a fifth and a third of guardsmen and reservists with five years of experience are predicted to change DMOS in any 15-month interval even if they do not change units.

Table 3.6

Predicted Percentage Changing DMOS During 15-Month
Interval by Years of Reserve Service
(assumes same unit FY86 and FY87)

Years of	Army National Guard		Army Reserve	
Service	NPS	PS	NPS	PS
1	14.28	14.23	23.12	20.40
2	13.68	13.89	21.39	19.62
3	13.11	13.58	19.87	18.91
4	12.59	13.29	18.53	18.27
5	12.11	13.03	17.36	17.68
6	11.65	12.78	16.34	17.16
7	11.24	12.56	15.46	16.68
8	10.85	12.36	14.70	16.26
9	10.49	12.17	14.06	15.89
10	10.16	12.01	13.52	15.56

Unit Characteristics and Job Change

Unit characteristics have more modest effects on DMOS change than individual characteristics. Table 3.7 shows that DMOS change is more common in larger units than in units with fewer than 51 members. In the Army Reserve, DMOS change is lowest for those units with fewer than 51 members, next lowest for large units with more than 200 members, and highest for units with 51 to 200 members.

We had expected that unit attrition or equipment modernization would relate positively to DMOS change, but neither variable is significant in the equation. High attrition could cause units to reassign personnel into shortage job areas, but there is no evidence that this is an important factor in DMOS change. Modernization could increase reassignment because previous jobs might become obsolete, but modernization also has no significant effect on DMOS turbulence after controlling for other factors.

For the most part, DMOS turbulence does not vary significantly with the mobilization status of an individual's unit. Individual USAR personnel in units with ALO priority 3 (80 percent of MTOE) have DMOS turbulence rates 12 to 16 percentage points higher than those with lower levels of MTOE.

Table 3.7

Differences in DMOS Change Percentages During 15-Month Interval by Unit Characteristics

Characteristic	Army National Guard		Army Reserve	
	NPS	PS	NPS	PS
Unit size				
51–100	4.28*	6.16*	16.57**	8.26**
101–150	3.14	5.87*	14.05**	8.98**
151–200	0.23	1.00	13.11**	11.73**
201 or more	5.29	7.86*	8.47*	7.67*
Unit attrition (%)				
YOS 1–4	0.02	–0.00	–0.06	0.00
YOS 5–9	–0.00	0.01	0.08*	0.00
YOS 10–19	–0.01	–0.01	0.12	–0.07
YOS 20 or more	–0.01	–0.00	0.04	0.05*
Series J TOE	0.12	–0.86	–1.92	1.34
mobilization status				
ALO-1	–4.88	0.40	2.32	0.67
ALO-2	–3.83	5.08	6.69	6.32
ALO-3	–1.53	7.46*	11.79*	15.80**
Unit type				
Combat	4.28**	1.74	–14.68**	–6.49
Combat support	3.22	2.34	–2.97	2.18

NOTE: The reference categories are unit size 1 to 50, TOE series other than J, ALO level lower than 3, and combat service support unit. Starred and double-starred entries are based on logistic regression coefficients that differ significantly from zero at the 5 and 1 percent confidence levels, respectively.

Nor does DMOS turbulence vary significantly with unit type—combat, combat support, and combat service support units have similar levels of DMOS turbulence after controlling for other individual and unit characteristics. There are a couple of exceptions. Nonprior-service guardsmen in combat units have change rates about 4 percentage points higher than those in combat service support units. Army Reserve personnel in combat units have change rates about 15 percentage points lower than those in combat service support units, but only 7 percent of USAR personnel are assigned to combat units.

SUMMARY OF ISSUES FOR CHANGING JOBS AND UNITS

Examination of the patterns of job and unit changes leads to the following general observations.

- **A significant number of reservists switch DMOS.**

One-fifth of the members of the National Guard and nearly one-third of the Army Reserve switched DMOS during the 15-month period. More unqualified personnel changed DMOS than qualified, and the most switches were from high-skill combat jobs.

- **Unit change is the most important factor in determining DMOS change.**

After 15 months, only 70 percent of the ARNG or USAR still hold the same job. Of the 30 percent leaving jobs, simple attrition accounts for 11 and 8 percent, respectively. Intracomponent unit changes account for the majority of the departures. Fifteen percent of the ARNG and 20 percent of the USAR join different units in their respective components. Cross-component transfers are less than 3 percent, and cross-service transfers are less than 1 percent. For members of the ARNG, 80 percent of those changing units change DMOS, and the figure is higher for the USAR, particularly if the change occurs to a unit within five miles of the original unit. Unit change has a similar effect on both prior- and nonprior-service reservists.

- **A significant amount of retraining occurs even for those who remain in the same unit.**

Somewhat surprisingly, even those remaining in the same unit face substantial job retraining. Twelve percent of the ARNG and 19 percent of the USAR members remaining in the same unit change DMOS and need retraining.

- **Reservists have a wide array of units to choose from.**

Most reservists have a number of units located near them. Within 50 miles of their homes, 90 percent of the Army Reserve and 84 percent of the National Guard have ten or more units to choose from. Less than 2 percent of either component have two or fewer units located within 50 miles.

- **Most unit switching appears to be voluntary.**

Two-thirds of the unit transfers take place between units located less than five miles apart. Transfers between units farther than 50 miles apart account for only 20 percent of the movements.

- **Individual job area affects DMOS change.**

As mentioned, prior unit change is the most important individual characteristic affecting DMOS change, and job qualification also has a significant effect. The particular job also makes a difference. Members of the Guard in noncombat skill jobs change more frequently.

- **Most unit characteristics do not seem to influence job switching.**

DMOS change is more common in large units than in small, but other characteristics such as attrition, mobilization status (ALO), modernization, and unit type do not seem to have a major, across-the-board effect. Some exceptions exist by category, for example, USAR personnel in combat units change DMOS less frequently.

Chapter Four

CHANGES IN QUALIFICATION RATES OVER TIME

Table 4.1 shows qualification rates at the beginning and end of the 15-month period for those remaining in the service. The remaining nonprior-service personnel have lower qualification rates than the starting group, but prior-service rates are slightly higher for the ARNG and about the same for the USAR. This indicates that the rate of retraining is slightly lower than the rate of DMOS change. The reserve components are retraining individuals at slightly lower rates than individuals are changing DMOS.

Table 4.2 shows the pervasive effect of job and unit turbulence on job qualification rates. The data show that only 29 percent of guardsmen and 19 percent of reservists who changed units and DMOS during the 15-month period were qualified at the end of the period. A higher percentage (slightly over 50 percent) of those who changed DMOS but not units were job qualified at the end of the period.

Table 4.1

**Longitudinal Changes in Skill Qualification for
the 1986 Reserve Components Survey
(FY87 qualification excludes attrition)**

	Percent Qualified	
Unit	June 1986	September 1987
ARNG		
Nonprior service	88	85
Prior service	77	80
USAR		
Nonprior service	80	73
Prior service	71	70

Table 4.2

**MOS Qualification Rate in September 1987 for Individuals
Changing Jobs and Units**

Status in 15-Month Period[a]	Percent Qualified (September 1987)	
	ARNG	USAR
Same DMOS, same unit	94	89
Same DMOS, different unit	89	84
Different DMOS, same unit	55	53
Different DMOS, different unit	29	19
Overall (excludes attrition)	83	71

[a]June 1986 to September 1987.

Changing both DMOS and unit has a slightly larger effect on qualification than simply changing DMOS in the same unit. Soldiers who change DMOS but stay in the same unit have FY87 qualification rates 5 percentage points higher than those who change DMOS and change units. Apparently, unit changes disrupt training coordination and lengthen the time required for qualification.

Table 4.2 also shows that 6 and 11 percent of ARNG and USAR soldiers who have neither changed DMOS nor units remain unqualified in FY87. Put another way, these reservists have not qualified in their jobs after more than 15 months.

Irrespective of job or unit change, the USAR qualification rate is always slightly less than that for ARNG. Overall, the USAR qualification rate for the survey cohort in FY87 is 12 percentage points lower than in the Guard. This difference reflects both the lower initial FY86 qualification rate and higher levels of DMOS turbulence in the USAR.

The remainder of this chapter examines the skill requalification patterns of two groups:

• Reservists changing DMOS between FY86 and F87 and

• Reservists who did not change DMOS but were unqualified in FY86.

The remaining group was qualified in FY86 and did not change DMOS, so by definition it is also qualified in FY87.

PATTERNS OF RETRAINING AND REQUALIFICATION FOR THOSE CHANGING DMOS

Table 4.3 shows the results from our recursive logit analysis of FY87 qualification status for reservists who changed DMOS between FY86 and FY87. The results indicate that requalification in a new skill was much slower for soldiers who had also changed units: Army guardsmen and reservists who changed units had qualification rates 20 and 30 percentage points lower, respectively, than those staying in the same unit. The data also show that requalification was slowest for those changing to nearby units—within five miles of the FY86 unit. These changes to nearby units were not driven by factors like reservist relocation, so one might expect that many of them would result in better job matches because the soldier found a position in his or her DMOS or a closely related MOS. In short, one would hope that unit switching within an area would tend to enhance the qualification status of units, but our evidence indicates that requalification is slower for personnel in local moves than for those moving more than 50 miles. Fine tuning of a job match is less possible for those moving longer distances because those moves are dictated by changes in the reservists' civilian career, and the job match is driven by what opportunities are available in the new area.

Changed residence has little effect on requalification status after controlling for whether the individual has changed units. Requalification is not affected by whether residential change caused the unit change. We had expected that residential relocations might lead to poor job matches because the reservist might be unable to find job openings in his skill in a new area. These poor matches would mean that retraining would take longer than if the reservist found a closely related job. The results suggest that many reservists are shopping for new jobs in their local area and changing units as positions become available. Requalification is slower for changes to nearby units because these changes are probably driven by reservist desire to change DMOS altogether. Such local DMOS changes may help morale and ultimately fill needed specialties, but the short-term effect of this local reserve turbulence is to depress reserve skill qualification levels.

The effect of FY86 qualification status on requalification differs considerably across components and prior-service groups. It is more

Table 4.3

Differences in Requalification Percentages for Reservists
Changing Duty Assignments

Characteristic	Army National Guard		Army Reserve	
	NPS	PS	NPS	PS
Pay grade				
E4	7.78	20.08*	6.40	12.25
E5	6.00	19.37*	−0.75	12.31
E6	5.37	13.00	−5.36	10.66
E7	4.08	12.38	−2.83	18.10
E8	36.38**	52.96**	30.10*	38.17**
E9	6.19	44.77	−24.44	0.66
Education/aptitude				
Nongraduate	−0.22	−11.10**	6.03	0.87
Education > 12 yr	2.76	0.02	7.15	4.64
AFQT Cat III	−4.29	4.06	0.64	−3.00
AFQT Cat IV, V	−5.91	7.10	4.71	−6.69
Retraining job area				
High skill	−0.03	2.84	31.57**	21.11**
Low skill	11.85**	5.76	11.63*	8.02*
Changed residence				
0 to 5 miles	−11.52*	6.88	−3.26	−4.36
6 to 50 miles	−0.87	−6.19	2.04	−5.23
> 50 miles	−1.57	−1.81	−1.41	−4.57
Changed unit				
0 to 5 miles	−26.13**	−22.49**	−36.53**	−35.57**
6 to 50 miles	−15.19**	−9.18	−17.01*	−18.70**
> 50 miles	−19.94**	−13.80**	−21.89**	−11.45*
Qualified 1986	20.78**	−14.44**	−1.33	−4.43
Changed pay grade	22.48**	25.77**	16.23**	17.19**
Changed component	−18.67**	−18.63**	13.62	9.14
Redesignated unit	−10.28	−0.85	14.09	19.64*

NOTE: The reference categories are E3, high school graduate, AFQT Category I or II, retrained combat skill, no residence change, no unit change, not duty qualified in FY86, no pay grade change, no component change, and unit not redesignated. Starred and double-starred entries are based on logistic regression coefficients that differ significantly from zero at the 5 and 1 percent confidence levels, respectively.

costly for a qualified reservist than an unqualified reservist to change DMOS, because the reserves must forgo the return on the training and experience of a qualified soldier. We saw in Chapter Three that qualified soldiers had reassignment rates 20 percentage points lower than unqualified soldiers. Among DMOS changes, one might expect a quicker requalification rate among those previously qualified both because initial qualification is some indication of the reservist's diligence and proficiency and because the Army Reserve may be more careful in organizing a retraining program before reassigning a qualified soldier.

The results for previous qualification status are mixed. The requalification rate for nonprior-service guardsmen is 21 percentage points higher for soldiers who were qualified in FY86 than for those who were not. The pattern is reversed, however, for prior-service guardsmen; previously qualified soldiers have qualification rates 14 percentage points lower than those not previously qualified. In the USAR, FY86 qualification status had no bearing on the requalification of reassigned reservists.

Changing component apparently retards requalification of ARNG personnel but has no significant effect on USAR personnel. Guardsmen who changed components had requalification rates 19 percentage points lower than those changing jobs within the Guard. This large difference occurs after controlling for other factors including unit change. There is no comparable effect for USAR personnel who join the Guard.

Requalified soldiers are much more likely to have been promoted (i.e., changed pay grades) between FY86 and FY87. Those promoted have requalification rates about 24 and 17 percentage points higher in the ARNG and USAR, respectively, than those who were not promoted during this period. The promotion "effect" on requalification should be interpreted cautiously, however, because our data do not allow us to assess whether the promotion occurred before or after the job reassignment or because of it. If promotion occurred before the reassignment, then the result would suggest that recently promoted reservists might be better motivated or have higher military aptitude so that they are able to requalify more quickly than reservists who were not recently promoted. In many cases, however, the promotion may occur after the reassignment, and in these cases promotion may be coincident with requalification because Army policy requires that a soldier be qualified in his assigned occupation at promotion.

Reservist pay grade has no consistent effect on requalification except for the E8 pay-grade level. E8s have very high rates of reassignment and become requalified in their new jobs much more quickly than other reservists. The more rapid requalification of these senior personnel probably reflects both the fact that they receive a lot of cross-training in closely related jobs and that they are more motivated to learn the new job than other reservists. The only other pay-grade effect is that guardsmen in pay grades E4 and E5 have requalification rates about 20 percentage points higher than those in pay grade E3.

Neither education nor aptitude had much effect on requalification. The only statistically significant effect is that the requalification rates of nongraduates are 11 percentage points lower than graduates for PS guardsmen.

Years of reserve service also have no significant effect on requalification (see Table A.4). Reservists are slightly less likely to be reassigned as YOS increases, but general reserve experience (YOS) does not translate into quicker requalification in new jobs. The insignificance of YOS for requalification means that the quasi-learning curve of Chapter Two is misleading. Indeed, the cross-sectional relationship between skill qualification and YOS occurs *because* the probability of job reassignment falls with YOS, and a quasi-learning curve from cross-sectional data will seriously misrepresent the propensity of more experienced personnel to learn new jobs more quickly than inexperienced personnel.

Requalification differs substantially by job area in the USAR but much less so in the Guard. In the USAR, requalification is quickest in high-skilled noncombat jobs, followed by low-skilled noncombat jobs, and finally combat jobs. For NPS personnel, the requalification rates are 32 and 12 percentage points higher in noncombat jobs, re-spectively, as compared with combat jobs. For PS personnel, the requalification rates are 21 and 8 percentage points higher in noncombat jobs, respectively, as compared with combat jobs. Requalification does not vary significantly with job area in the Guard except that NPS personnel in low-skilled noncombat jobs have re-qualification rates about 12 percentage points higher than those in other job areas.

LONG-TERM QUALIFICATION PROBLEMS: QUALIFICATION PATTERNS AMONG THOSE UNQUALIFIED IN FY86 AND NOT CHANGING JOBS

Some reservists apparently have chronic job qualification problems. Among the recruits in our sample who were unqualified in FY86 and did not change jobs, the FY87 qualification rate was only 56 percent in the ARNG and 48 percent in the USAR. These rates are surprisingly low after 15 months of assignment and (presumably) training in the FY86 job. The rates seem particularly low when compared with the qualification rates of 55 and 53 percent in the ARNG and USAR for reservists who were reassigned to a new DMOS in the same unit during this time period. The low rates of qualification for continuously assigned soldiers indicate chronic problems that make it difficult for some soldiers to receive and complete adequate training in their assigned MOS.

Table 4.4 shows the results from the logistic analysis of patterns in DMOS qualification for reservists unqualified in FY86 and not reassigned to a different DMOS. In general, the logistic regression results are disappointing because they provide little insight into the qualification patterns of this group.

The only consistently significant variable is change in pay grade, that is, a promotion during the period. As discussed for those who change jobs, this coefficient may simply reflect the fact that Army policy requires that individuals are assigned in their PMOS at the time of promotion.

The coefficients associated with other variables are almost all insignificant. A potential explanation for the low qualification rates of this group would be that they are disproportionately assigned to occupations with very long training times. The results do not support this explanation. Prior-service guardsmen in technical noncombat jobs do have qualification rates 21 percent lower than those in combat skills, but in general, there is little difference in qualification by reservist job area.

The persistently low qualification rate for those continuously assigned to the same job remains a mystery. Several explanations are possible. Perhaps some of these reservists are not seriously pursuing their training and are planning to leave the reserves. Some may be assigned in areas where they lack access to facilities needed to complete their training. Others may be languishing in units where they are not provided with adequate time or encouragement to finish their training. Still others may have had their training interrupted by a job reassignment and then been reassigned back to their FY86 skill. Unfortunately, the database is not rich enough to sort among these and a variety of other competing explanations.

Table 4.4

Differences in FY87 Qualification Percentages for Reservists Who Were Unqualified in FY86 and Did Not Change Duty Assignments During 15-Month Interval

	Army National Guard		Army Reserve	
Characteristic	NPS	PS	NPS	PS
Pay grade				
E4	19.47*	10.82	−1.79	8.66
E5	22.61*	8.84	−4.51	9.69
E6	16.58	8.39	−11.15	13.49
E7	17.97	13.22	−19.44	18.47
E8	14.88	−2.24	−9.48	15.01
E9	28.42	32.14	−0.41	41.75*
Education/aptitude				
Nongraduate	−10.44	−3.18	2.61	−0.95
Education > 12	−12.38*	−11.04*	1.66	−1.22
AFQT Cat III	−1.83	−0.93	−5.42	4.48
AFQT Cat IV, V	11.77	2.24	−21.85*	1.38
Job area				
High skill	−6.81	−21.41**	−5.82	−1.90
Low skill	−1.59	−7.28	0.65	−0.89
Changed residence				
0 to 5 miles	17.68*	6.61	10.34	8.27
6 to 50 miles	8.65	10.76	21.40*	−1.51
> 50 miles	−1.97	−16.91	−14.04	8.12
Changed unit				
0 to 5 miles	4.45	−1.32	17.17	2.19
6 to 50 miles	−12.35	2.86	43.42*	20.38
> 50 miles	−13.59	6.40	5.96	3.76
Changed pay grade	33.05**	32.71**	27.60**	24.80**
Changed component	7.36	−14.65	11.71	0.34
Redesignated unit	−1.23	−24.70*	−18.02	8.47

NOTE: The reference categories are E3, high school graduate, AFQT Category I or II, trained combat skill, no residence change, no unit change, no pay-grade change, no component change, and unit not redesignated. Starred and double-starred entries are based on logistic regression coefficients that differ significantly from zero at the 5 and 1 percent confidence levels, respectively.

SUMMARY OF ISSUES FOR CHANGES IN QUALIFICATION RATES

- **The effect of DMOS turbulence on qualification levels is large enough to offset the increase of soldiers qualifying in their DMOS.**

Perhaps the most telling effect of job turbulence is that it offsets any gains in qualification made through the various training programs. Thus, at best, unit qualification levels can only hold constant. Given the amount of resources devoted to training, turbulence is exacting a substantial price.

- **The USAR suffers consistently lower qualification levels than the ARNG.**

This difference stems from the fact that the USAR begins with a lower qualification rate and experiences greater job turbulence.

Considering reassigned soldiers, the data suggest that:

- **Many reservists search among units for jobs.**

We draw this conclusion based on the facts that most unit moves are between battalions and within five miles of the previous unit and thus are probably not directed, and changing residence does not seem to generate unit moves. Reservists also have a number of in-centives to move, including promotion and more desirable jobs.

- **Those who do change units requalify in a new MOS slower than those who change jobs within the same unit.**

This effect may result from soldiers switching to entirely new jobs or integrating into training programs more slowly than those who change jobs within the same units.

- **The effect of reassignments on MOSQ is worse for nearby units than those farther away.**

Somewhat surprisingly, it takes longer to requalify soldiers who move to nearby units. One would think that soldiers moving to far-away units would have less selection, suffer greater MOS mismatch, and thus face longer retraining times. That appears not to be the case.

For those who were unqualified in FY87, we find:

- **A significant number of soldiers remain unqualified in their DMOS after 15 months of training.**

The data indicate that some soldiers have long-term difficulty be-coming qualified in their DMOS. In fact, soldiers who were unqualified in FY87 do not fare any better than soldiers who changed jobs during the period.

- **The only variable that correlates with qualification is promotion.**

The data show that promotion and qualification correlate positively. The data do not show the specific reason for this correlation. It could result from motivated soldiers working hard to achieve a higher rank or an administrative feature of the promotion system that automatically awards qualification with the new rank.

Chapter Five

ESTIMATES OF JOB RETRAINING TIMES

Chapter Three showed a relatively high level of DMOS change among both qualified and unqualified reservists, and Chapter Four examined the amount of retraining that occurred. This chapter estimates how long that job retraining takes. To answer that question, we must look at those who began retraining in the 15-month time period. Overall, the data in Table 5.1 show that 20 percent of guardsmen (3246/16,038) and 32 percent of reservists (2529/7987) in our sample started retraining during the 15-month period. Approximately one-third of this retraining requirement arises from individuals who were not duty qualified in June 1986 but switched to a second job. To measure job training time, we must examine the percentage of those starting retraining who finish by the end of the period. If a high

Table 5.1

Training Status Groups for the Army National Guard and Reserve

Qualification Status on June 1, 1986	Job Change Status 6/86 to 9/87		
	No Change in DMOS	Change in DMOS	Total
National Guard			
Qualified	11,178	2,295	13,473
Not qualified	1,614	951	2,565
Total	12,792	3,246	16,038
Army Reserve			
Qualified	4,411	1,609	6,020
Not qualified	1,047	920	1,967
Total	5,458	2,529	7,987

percentage are retrained by the end of the period, training times will be short. If a low percentage of individuals are retrained by the end of the period, training times will be long.

Table 5.2 shows the percentage of individuals completing training by September 1987. About one-third of the previously qualified group has requalified by the end of the period. For the previously unqualified group, one-third of reservists and one-half of guardsmen have requalified by September 1987.

The higher requalification rate for the latter group might be explained by two hypotheses. The first is that the group contains some individuals who were waiting for jobs for which they were previously trained to become available. These individuals would have short training times and bias the requalification estimate upward. Alternatively, it might be hypothesized that individuals in this group were more likely to start retraining early in the period. If so, they would be more likely to finish before the end of the period. They would probably begin earlier because they may be more likely to be shifted out of jobs closer to the beginning of training than the end. These data show that some skill switching may be to jobs for which individuals were previously qualified.

In estimating training times, we will concentrate on the members of the group who were qualified in FY86 and switched sometime during the period. These individuals are likely to start retraining randomly during that time. If this assumption is correct, and if we also assume that all training times are less than 15 months and that the

Table 5.2

**Percentage of Reservists Reassigned in 15-Month Interval
Who Completed Training by September 1987**

	National Guard	Army Reserve
Duty qualified in 6/86	37.0	33.7
Not duty qualified in 6/86	50.5	35.4

same distribution of training times exists for each month,[1] then the average retraining time can be expressed as a simple function of the proportion of soldiers who finish by the end of the period:

$$T = 15 - 15p$$

where T = average retraining time in months

p = proportion completing training by September 1987.

If we assume that all individuals have training times of six months, then those who start by month nine of the period will complete training, while those starting later will not finish. If we have uniform input over the 15-month period, the proportion finishing training will be 9/15.

RESULTS FOR JOB RETRAINING TIMES

Figure 5.1 provides estimated job retraining times by component and prior-service status. The data show average skill retraining time to be between nine and ten months, with slightly longer time for the Army Reserve and prior-service personnel. This retraining time is probably biased downward because undoubtedly some retraining takes longer than 15 months. Figure 5.2 shows that job retraining times vary markedly by the retraining job. Combat jobs in both the Guard and Reserve take an average of 12.5 months to requalify, whereas non-combat jobs usually take between six and nine months. Among non-combat jobs, high-skilled jobs appear to take a little over a month longer than low-skilled jobs in the Guard. However, in the Army Reserve there appears to be much faster retraining times for high-skilled as opposed to low-skilled jobs.

---

[1]A revised database currently under discussion could track individuals quarterly over longer time periods and test these assumptions explicitly. This would be beneficial because the estimated retraining times are moderately sensitive to the accuracy of these assumptions.

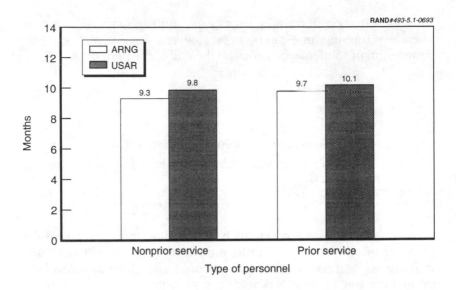

Figure 5.1—Average Retraining Time by Component and
Prior-Service Status

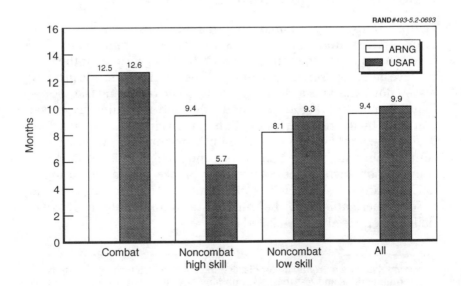

Figure 5.2—Average Job Retraining Times for Different Jobs

The longer training times for combat jobs might arise from the need for field practice and testing of skills, as opposed to noncombat jobs that can be learned and practiced more often at the Armory. Since reserve units go to combat training grounds only four to six times a year, this limited opportunity for training might considerably lengthen the time involved in retraining. An alternative explanation is that combat training may be better structured—with better testing and higher proficiency required—either because of increased priority or the increased risk of accident and equipment damage in combat jobs.

We also explored whether training time depended on the previous job. The hypothesis here is that retraining in a similar job will take less time than in a dissimilar job. Figures 5.3 and 5.4 show job retraining times for both initial and final jobs. The dominant influence is still the final job, although there is some evidence that retraining from high-skilled jobs to other high-skilled jobs is shorter than from combat or low-skilled jobs.

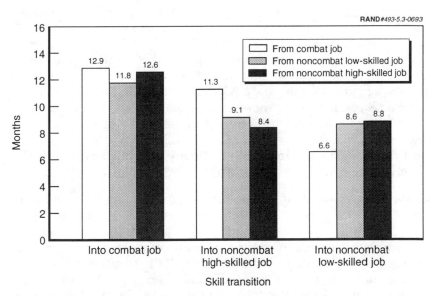

Figure 5.3—Average Job Retraining Time by Initial and Final Job: ARNG

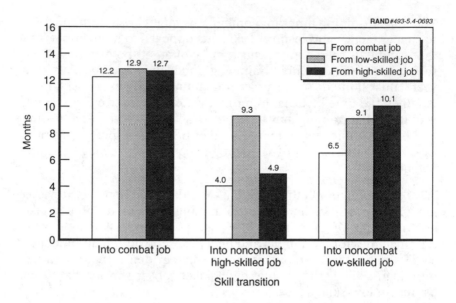

Figure 5.4—Average Job Retraining Time by Initial and Final Job: USAR

We have some evidence concerning the distribution of training times. A narrow distribution means that most people take close to the average time to train, and a wide distribution indicates that many people take significantly more or less than the average time. The sample of individuals who were not qualified in 1986 and did not switch jobs have been retraining for a minimum of 15 months. We find that only 55.8 percent in the Guard and 48.4 percent in the Reserve have qualified by the end of the period.

These figures indicate the many reservists' retraining takes substantially longer than the average retraining time of 9–10 months. This wide distribution may indicate substantial differences in unit priority and emphasis, in quality and priority among those retraining or in standards for accepting job qualification. If the reason is differences in unit priority or emphasis or individual priority, management emphasis or individual and unit incentives might be effective in addressing the problem. If the reason is difference in standards for different units, enforcing more uniform and rigid standards may significantly decrease reservists' training times.

SUMMARY OF ISSUES RELATING TO RETRAINING TIME

Analysis of the data pertaining to retraining time leads to four major observations:

- The average retraining time for all jobs is nine to ten months.

- Retraining in combat jobs requires significantly more time, 12.5 months on average.

- A soldier's previous job does not seem to influence retraining time.

- Many reservists take substantially longer than the average of nine to ten months to retrain.

Chapter Six

CONCLUSIONS AND RECOMMENDATIONS

RESULTS

The major results of our study fall into the following areas:

- Qualification differences among ARNG and USAR personnel and units

- Causes of unqualified personnel among E3 to E9 personnel

  — The relationship between qualification and changes in DMOS and units

  — Retraining required for entering prior-service personnel

  — Long retraining times for new DMOS.

Qualification Status of the Army Reserve Components

Soldiers not minimally qualified in their assigned MOS severely degrade the readiness of units in the Army Guard and Army Reserve. Approximately 16 percent of E3 to E9 personnel in the Guard and 25 percent of Army Reserve personnel were not qualified in June 1986. The rates of unqualified personnel are much higher for prior-service personnel and those in noncombat skills. Nonprior-service personnel had unqualified rates in the Guard and Reserve of 12 percent and 20 percent, respectively, compared with 23 and 29 percent for prior-service personnel. Combat jobs in the Guard had unqualified rates of only 7 percent compared with 25 percent for noncombat high-skilled jobs and 19 percent for noncombat low-skilled jobs. In the

Army Reserve, combat jobs had only slightly lower unqualified rates of 22 percent compared with 26 percent for high-skilled jobs and 25 percent for low-skilled jobs.

Causes of Unqualified Personnel Among E3 to E9 Personnel

In trying to determine why the qualification rate is so low among E3 to E9 personnel, we considered a number of possible causes including introduction of new equipment, migration of reservists resulting from civilian job changes, frequent changes in units and DMOS, retraining of prior-service accessions at entrance, and long requalification times. We find the main causes of unqualified personnel is the frequent retraining of prior-service accessions because of a lack of job matching with their active PMOS and frequent voluntary changes in units and components for both prior- and nonprior-service personnel that lead to a change in DMOS and long retraining times.

About 50 to 60 percent of entering prior-service personnel need retraining because their reserve DMOS does not match their previous active-duty DMOS. Some of this MOS mismatch is unavoidable because prior-service personnel chose geographical locations based on civilian job opportunities or personnel preference, and the choice of reserve MOS will be limited to local units that may not have jobs or availability for the particular MOS. However, some of the mismatch may occur because individuals do not fully search all available units for appropriate matches or simply prefer to change DMOS. Some may occur because of timing—job openings do not correspond with when individuals choose to join. We discuss below some policy options for addressing some of these problems.

Reservists change DMOS frequently once in the component. We find that over a 15-month period, 21 percent of E3 to E9 personnel in the Guard and 32 percent in the Army Reserve change DMOS. DMOS switching from combat skills is less frequent. This high rate of switching means that the original IADT or SOJT investment from previous training is lost. After five years in the reserves, only one-half of nonprior-service enlistees are in their original IADT PMOS. For prior-service personnel after five years in the reserves, only 20 percent are in their original active-duty MOS.

Most DMOS switching occurs in conjunction with unit switching. Unit switching is not primarily a result of geographical migration of reservists, but is rather voluntary switching among local units. Eighty percent of unit switches occur among units less than 50 miles apart. Over 80 percent of reservists have a choice of ten or more units within 50 miles of their home. There is strong evidence in the Guard that switching is driven primarily by promotion, whereas for the Reserve changing to more desirable skills may play an important role.

Changing units is more prevalent among prior-service personnel. Within six years of entry, about 50–60 percent of prior-service accessions have switched units. For nonprior-service accessions, 25–40 percent have switched units. Switching units is much more common in the Army Reserve than in the Guard. The combination of switching units and/or switching DMOS leaves only 62 percent of ARNG and 56 percent of USAR E3 to E9 personnel in the same unit and same DMOS after 15 months.

Equipment modernization and unit structure changes appeared not to be a major cause of disqualification. This may be due to the infrequency of such changes in the FY86 and FY87 time period or because retraining occurs faster for these units. It may also be the case that we have not captured all of these changes in the current database. We have measured unit changes through identifying Series J MTOE units. We have also identified units who changed Unit Identification Code (UIC) in the period. A closer examination of these methods is required for reserve personnel to determine whether the methods capture all of the changes in requirements and equipment.

We have found no differences in MOS qualification levels as a result of units being in ALO-1 category. More combat service and service support units are in this category, and these types of units have somewhat lower qualification levels than combat units. However, controlling for type of unit, there appears to be no increase in MOS qualification for ALO-1 units. Either the additional resources provided do not affect qualification levels or few additional resources are provided as a result of being in an ALO-1 status.

Qualification rates will be lower the longer it takes to retrain personnel through SOJT. We have developed an estimate of the average retraining times for reservists by tracking individuals who changed DMOS and either did or did not requalify by the end of the 15-month period. Improved data that track individuals over longer time periods would considerably improve these estimates. The present estimates show average retraining times of between nine and ten months for both the Guard and Army Reserve. However, combat MOS take considerably longer to retrain than noncombat MOS. Combat MOS take 12–13 months whereas noncombat MOS take 6–9 months. In the active force, combat MOS have the shortest training times. The difference might be explained by the need for field training and testing and the fact that Reserve combat units go to the field only four to six times a year. Alternatively, combat retraining may be more structured and tighter quality control exercised for a variety of reasons—some related to risk of personnel injury or equipment damage.

INITIAL RECOMMENDATIONS AND POTENTIAL FUTURE RESEARCH

Given these results, what actions should policymakers take to address these issues? Our recommendations fall into two broad areas: those that promote a better job match and those that work to reduce the amount of job and unit changing that goes on by stabilizing personnel in their jobs.

From a policy perspective, it is important to determine whether the training loads are primarily driven by voluntary decisions or by component decisions. In the case of prior-service accessions, one would like to know whether the individual had a choice of joining units that could use his or her previous PMOS. We know from the present analysis that almost all reservists have a wide choice of available units. How thoroughly does the individual search among units? If the job search were complete, would it result in a job match with previous jobs? Or does the individual prefer to change into a new job upon joining the Reserve?

Recommendations to Promote a Better Job Match

- **Change bonus policies to reward job matching at entry and job longevity once in the force.**

Under the current prior-service bonus system, the individual has no incentive to search for a job match with existing skills among all local units, and there is no way for a reservist to wait until appropriate jobs open up. We should be willing to pay higher bonuses to prior-service individuals who use active PMOS in the reserves because we do not have to pay retraining costs. We might also create temporary positions for individuals with the appropriate job PMOS where it is probable that an MOS matching the active PMOS will open within three to six months. Currently, such an individual usually starts retraining for a new position rather than await a position for which no retraining is required. We should also make downstream payments for enlistment and reenlistment bonus payments conditional on spending a minimum time in the current job.

- **Evaluate the possibility of centralized local recruiting and reserve component employment information across all components to ease job matching and to monitor interunit and intercomponent transfers.**

Competition between components and units for prior-service personnel may also play a role in low levels of job matches. Units have no incentive to refer individuals to other units to create better job matches. A more centralized and cooperative local reserve component recruiting network for prior-service personnel could result in the individual obtaining better information on reserve component positions and better matches of people to jobs for reserve component units.

The Department of Defense should evaluate the costs and benefits of a local area reserve component employment and information service. Component data on current vacancies could be pooled to provide information to prospective prior-service recruits and those in the internal labor market. It would provide better information to prospective recruits and help channel individuals to utilize previous skills. It would also serve as a clearinghouse for individuals seeking unit or component changes. Historical data on reservists in the area could be available to check on job longevity, length of service, and eligibility to change jobs and components. It could also provide the basis for better regulation of unit changes to minimize retraining.

Policies to Reduce Job and Unit Switching

- **Make "simple" modifications to the reserve component pay table that would extend or increase longevity increments and reduce promotion incentive.**

Several policies could be effective in deterring job changes. First, it is important to recognize that an important motivation for switching comes from the current reserve component pay table and from the TOE structure of reserve component units. The reserve component pay table—because it mirrors the active pay table—provides strong incentive for promotion rather than longevity. A typical E5 will receive an immediate 10 percent increase upon promotion and a 3 percent increase for serving two more years in the current grade. Moreover, many reservists stay in grade so long that they no longer receive longevity increments. This means that the only route to higher pay is promotion. Since retirement pay is linked to active pay, it is also substantially boosted through the promotion process.

- **Initiate proficiency pay for reservists.**

Changing the reserve component pay table may face serious political and practical obstacles. However, proficiency pay could provide many of the same advantages. Proficiency pay was once used in the active force to reward job proficiency and provide pay for individuals who preferred to stay in place and develop higher job proficiency rather than be promoted into positions requiring supervisory or administrative responsibilities. Reserve proficiency pay would be paid for longevity in a job and could be varied across units and jobs. It would provide additional pay the longer an individual stayed in a particular MOS. It would reduce the monetary incentive associated with promotions and work to keep individuals in their jobs longer.

- **Prudently change MTOE to make higher grade progression possible within certain jobs that are difficult to fill or require longer training times.**

Today's promotion-oriented system is exacerbated by a TOE authorization structure that limits the maximum pay grade achievable for a job. Many skills have ceilings on how many people can hold the higher pay grades. Further advancement means either waiting for a vacancy or switching jobs, and the latter is frequently the faster route. We thus have an incentive system that encourages individuals to seek higher pay grades as a route to higher pay, and to achieve higher pay grades by switching jobs.

This pay table and TOE structure serve the active component better than the reserves. Active forces need a higher grade structure and more senior careerists to man the more extensive training base and administrative structure of active forces. Active members pursue job retraining full-time and can complete it more quickly and surely than the reserves. The reserves need an incentive system that pays individuals to stay in jobs longer. Ideally, this would mean a redesigned pay table that could provide the same or higher pay to reservists but would provide less incentive for promotion and more incentive—in the form of higher and longer longevity increments—to stay in current jobs. The authorization structure could also be changed to allow higher grade progression for certain skills. Basically, we need to design a career incentive system for the reserves that keeps individuals in skills for five or ten or twenty years, depending on the type of skill.

- **Establish minimum job tenure periods to recoup training investment.**

Establishing minimum lengths of service within a skill before transfers are possible would reduce job switching. Exceptions for geographical migration could be provided. Transfers between components should be more strongly regulated to ensure that training investment is protected. The role of competition between components for personnel should be examined.

- **Regulate intercomponent and intraunit transfers to protect job investment.**

Changing units appears to be by reservists' choice. Much could be done to reduce the training load arising from these transfers. Reservists behave in the internal labor market much like in the civilian labor market. They shop for better jobs and switch once they find them. Better jobs mean higher pay grades or preferred jobs or units. Other jobs might be preferred because of status, civilian transferability, or compatibility with civilian work schedules or family time. Reservists are quite active in these internal job searches, and almost all reservists have a wide choice of available units. Current component and DoD policies neither restrain nor discourage such voluntary moves. Thus, substantial investments made in training are not protected or recouped, and increased training resources become necessary.

AREAS OF FURTHER RESEARCH

This research has raised several questions that require policy evaluation, policy initiative, or further research:

- How do we prudently redesign MTOE structure for reserve component units to keep individuals in jobs longer?

- Are "simple" modifications to the reserve component pay table like extended longevity payments politically and economically feasible?

- How effective would proficiency pay be in keeping individuals in their jobs?

- How can we impose minimum job tenure rules without suffering undue attrition losses?

- Would tighter regulation of unit and component transfers result in increased attrition?

- How do we regulate intercomponent transfers to protect training investment and minimize attrition?

- How effective would additional bonus payments be for prior-service personnel to find matching reserve component MOS?

- How effective would enlistment and reenlistment bonus payments be if longer job commitments are required?

- How do we design a reserve component "career" to keep individuals in the same jobs for ten or fifteen or twenty years?

This analysis used data from FY86 and FY87—three years before Operation Desert Storm. Evidence from Desert Storm mobilization indicates that many reserve component personnel were non-deployable because they were not MOS qualified. Additional analysis with more recent data could determine whether there have been changes in qualification levels. We have analyzed only the Army components. Determining and comparing qualification and turbulence levels across all reserve components would provide additional evidence as to the causes. Comparison with active-duty levels would also be interesting since the assumption that all active units have fully qualified personnel may not be accurate. Finally, survey data directed to understanding the causes of unit switching would provide a much clearer picture of individual motivation for such action.

STATISTICAL MODEL

The statistical model used to analyze patterns of skill qualification and turbulence is the recursive logit model (Maddala, 1983; Lee, 1981; Schmidt and Strauss, 1975). This econometric model links the qualification and turbulence information into a unified framework. We have three equations: one for duty qualification in June 1986 (Q86 = 1 if qualified, 0 otherwise), one for changed duty assignment between June 1986 and October 1987 (ΔDMOS = 1 for changed jobs, 0 otherwise), and one for duty qualification in October 1987 (Q87 = 1 if qualified, 0 otherwise). The model is recursive and sequential: Q86 is determined first, ΔDMOS is determined next and is conditional on Q86, and, finally, Q87 is conditional on both Q86 and ΔDMOS. Let X_1 be a set of variables affecting Q86, X_2 be a set of variables affecting ΔDMOS, and X_3 be a set of variables affecting Q87. The model specification is expressed in log odds ratio form as follows:

Q86: $\quad ln\left[P\left(Q86_i = 1\right)/P\left(Q86_i = 0\right)\right] = X_{1i}\,\beta_1,$

ΔDMOS: $\quad ln\left[P\left(\Delta DMOS_i = 1\right)/P\left(\Delta DMOS_i = 0\right)\right] = X_{2i}\,\beta_2 + \alpha Q86_i,$

Q87: $\quad ln\left[P\left(Q87_i = 1\right)/P\left(Q87_i = 0\right) \mid \Delta DMOS = 1\right] = X_{3i}\,\beta_3 + \gamma\,Q86_i,$

$\quad ln\left[P\left(Q87_i = 1\right)/P\left(Q87_i = 0\right) \mid \Delta DMOS = 0 \text{ and } Q86 = 0\right] = X_{3i}\,\beta_4,$

where P(.) represents the probability of the event occurring; β_1, β_2, β_3, and β_4 are vectors of unknown parameters; α and γ are unknown parameters; and i indexes the individual reservist observations. The

73

Q86 equation is a snapshot of what factors affect qualification at one point in time. This snapshot provides useful information on what types of individuals are likely to be qualified or what unit characteristics are associated with high levels of individual skill qualification. In a static world, the Q86 equation could also provide estimates of time required for learning an occupational skill. Learning curves can be estimated from the relationship between years of reserve service (YOS) and Q86, but these curves are misleading if individuals do not remain continuously assigned to a single specialty.[1] Suppose that after adjusting for other factors, for example, the qualification level at one year was 70 percent and at two years was 80 percent. If members of a year group were not reassigned between the first and second year, we could infer that 10 percent of a year group become qualified between the first and second year. In our database, however, we do not know whether unqualified reservists in June 1986 were continuously assigned in their current specialty since the time of their reserve accession, so we can only infer the increase in qualification rates for a year group net of the decrement in qualification rates associated with job reassignment. If reassignment is common, then the learning curves estimated from a cross-section or snapshot in time will under-estimate the speed at which a continuously assigned reservist would become skill qualified.

The job reassignment equation provides insights into what types of factors are associated with job reassignment. Some reassignment is inevitable because of skill shortages or surpluses and residential relocation of reservists. Reserve policies may also encourage retraining because promotion opportunities may be limited in the reservist's initial skill or because cross-training is needed in a related skill. The α parameter of the job reassignment equation indicates whether qualified soldiers are more or less likely to be reassigned. Other things equal, it is more costly to lose the training investment in

---

[1]The learning curves from the Q86 equation may also be misleading because of a selection bias associated with reserve attrition. The bias would occur if the learning curve for those who remain in the reserves was unrepresentative of the learning curve for all cohort entrants. Those leaving the reserves might have taken longer to become skill qualified than those who chose to stay, so an attrition bias would lead us to underestimate the training time required for a group of entrants.

a skill-qualified soldier than to reassign an unqualified soldier to a new job, so we expect α to be negative.

FY87 qualification status is examined separately for two groups: those who have changed jobs and those who remained in the same job but were unqualified in FY86. β_3 and β_4 would be very similar if factors affecting the short-term requalification of reservists were similar to those affecting longer-term qualification of individuals who remain in a skill. Alternatively, continuously assigned reservists with chronic qualification problems might be assigned to skills with long training times or in units with late deployment dates. A third group of recruits was qualified in FY86 and did not change jobs between FY86 and FY87, but this group of recruits is qualified in FY87 by definition.

The Q87 requalification equation provides our best estimates of the effect of reassignment on qualification and on the learning curve for becoming qualified in a new skill. How likely are soldiers reassigned between FY86 and FY87 to be qualified in FY87? Reassignment in a closely related skill or a skill with a short training time might have a small effect on qualification. If retraining time is protracted, however, reassigned soldiers might take some time to become requalified in their new skills though an OJT program. How does the reassignment effect on FY87 qualification differ depending on FY86 qualification status? Our hypothesis is that $\gamma > 0$; that is, reassigned soldiers who were qualified in FY86 are more likely to be qualified in FY87 than reassigned soldiers who were unqualified in FY86, because unobserved factors like individual aptitude or dedication that affect FY86 qualification will have a similar effect on FY87 qualification.

Estimating the last equation illuminates factors that enhance the probability that a recruit assigned to the same skill for a year is likely to become qualified in that skill. This equation will allow us to identify whether there are certain individual or unit characteristics that affect the long-term potential of a recruit to become qualified in his assigned skill.

Table A.1

Definitions of Regression Variables

Individual's Background Variable	Definition
TIMEUN	Time in current unit (FY86) for those who changed unit before the survey; 0 for those not changing units
TIMEUN2	timeun*timeun
DIFFUN	Individual changed unit before survey in FY86
DIFFUNM	Changed unit is missing
YOS	Years of reserve service (YOS) in the FY86 survey
YOS2	yos*yos
PG	Pay grade in FY86
FORMSERV	Train for FY86 primary military occupational specialty (PMOS) in service school
OJTACT	On-the-job training for FY86 PMOS in active Army
HSNC86	High-skilled noncombat job in FY86
LSNC86	Low-skilled noncombat job in FY86
HSNC87	High-skilled noncombat job in FY87
LSNC87	Low-skilled noncombat job in FY87
DQUAL86	Duty qualified in FY86
DQUAL87	Duty qualified in FY87
Education/Aptitude	
NHSG	Nonhigh school graduate
HSPLUS	Education > 12 yr
HSG	Excluded reference category for high school graduates
CAT12	Excluded reference category for Armed Forces Qualification Test (AFQT)
CAT3	AFQT Category 3
CAT45	AFQT Categories 4 or 5
CATM	AFQT category missing
Unit Characteristics (FY86 Unit)	
SIZE100	Unit size 51 to 100
SIZE150	Unit size 101 to 150
SIZE200	Unit size 151 to 200
SIZE200P	Unit size greater than 200
ATT14	YOS 1 to 4 attrition percentage
ATT59	YOS 5 to 9 attrition percentage
ATT1019	YOS 10 to 19 attrition percentage
ATT20P	YOS 20 or more attrition percentage

Table A.1—continued

Individual's Background Variable	Definition
SERIESJ	Unit has J series Table of Organization and Equipment (TOE)
TIMEJ	Time with series J; 0 for units without series J
ALO1	ALO is required at 100 percent of MTOE
ALO2	ALO is required at 90 percent of MTOE
ALO3	ALO is required at 80 percent of MTOE
ALOX	Excluded reference category for ALO required less than 80 percent of MTOE
ALOM	ALO for unit is missing
COMBAT	Combat unit in FY86
COMSUP	Combat support unit in FY86
Status Changes During 15-Month Interval from FY86 to FY87	
HD05	Relocation to home within 5 miles
HD550	Relocation to home within 5 to 50 miles
HDGT50	Relocation to home 50 miles away
UD05	Relocation to unit within 5 miles
UD550	Relocation to unit within 5 to 50 miles
UDGT50	Relocation to unit 50 miles away
CHPG	Change in pay grade
CHDMOS	Changed duty military occupational specialty (DMOS)
NEWCOMP	Changed component
REDESIGN	Redesignated or new Army unit
AREA	Changed occupational area
GROUP	Changed occupational group
SUBGROUP	Changed occupational subgroup

Table A.2

**Logistic Regression Results for FY86 Duty Qualification in the
Army National Guard and Army Reserve
(standard errors in parentheses)**

Variable	Army National Guard		Army Reserve	
	NPS	PS	NPS	PS
INTERCEP	4.087**	1.816**	2.371**	−0.170**
TIMEUN	0.289**	0.184**	0.263**	0.135**
	(0.032)	(0.024)	(0.047)	(0.030)
TIMEUN2	−0.009**	−0.006**	−0.010**	−0.001
	(0.002)	(0.001)	(0.003)	(0.002)
DIFFUN	−2.062**	−1.125**	−1.704**	−1.153**
	(0.125)	(0.092)	(0.155)	(0.108)
DIFFUNM	0.032	0.006	−0.156	0.096
	(0.174)	(0.135)	(0.255)	(0.160)
YOS	−0.068**	0.139**	−0.044	0.168**
	(0.021)	(0.015)	(0.033)	(0.021)
YOS2	0.001	−0.004**	0.001	−0.006**
	(0.001)	(0.001)	(0.001)	(0.001)
PG4	0.184+	0.242	0.164	0.661**
	(0.104)	(0.197)	(0.142)	(0.202)
PG5	0.414**	0.458*	0.347+	0.950**
	(0.134)	(0.197)	(0.179)	(0.210)
PG6	0.373*	0.513*	0.391	1.014**
	(0.179)	(0.207)	(0.239)	(0.222)
PG7	0.430+	0.604**	0.042	0.951**
	(0.237)	(0.233)	(0.278)	(0.241)
PG8	0.661*	0.599*	0.111	0.376
	(0.324)	(0.294)	(0.347)	(0.282)
PG9	−0.508	0.972+	−0.569	1.431**
	(0.526)	(0.512)	(0.594)	(0.392)
FORMSERV	0.301**	0.288**	0.215*	0.191**
	(0.071)	(0.064)	(0.094)	(0.068)
OJTACT	0.347**	0.091	−0.062	0.291**
	(0.099)	(0.074)	(0.137)	(0.081)
NHSG	−0.027	0.058	0.046	−0.037
	(0.082)	(0.076)	(0.127)	(0.099)
HSPLUS	−0.110	−0.154*	−0.107	−0.083
	(0.083)	(0.070)	(0.103)	(0.077)
CAT3	−0.030	0.050	0.254*	0.292**
	(0.080)	(0.069)	(0.100)	(0.074)
CAT45	0.126	0.277+	0.074	0.487**
	(0.147)	(0.147)	(0.156)	(0.122)
CATM	0.196	−0.084		
	(0.142)	(0.089)		

Table A.2—continued

Variable	Army National Guard		Army Reserve	
	NPS	PS	NPS	PS
SIZE100	−0.038	−0.359**	−0.164	−0.196+
	(0.135)	(0.118)	(0.152)	(0.107)
SIZE150	0.000	−0.309**	−0.074	−0.010
	(0.135)	(0.119)	(0.158)	(0.114)
SIZE200	0.163	−0.339**	0.053	−0.059
	(0.145)	(0.125)	(0.166)	(0.121)
SIZE200P	0.199	−0.298+	−0.004	0.017
	(0.192)	(0.154)	(0.173)	(0.125)
ATT14	−0.001	−0.002	−0.006*	−0.002+
	(0.002)	(0.002)	(0.003)	(0.001)
ATT59	0.001	0.000	0.000	−0.000
	(0.002)	(0.002)	(0.002)	(0.001)
ATT1019	0.001	−0.003	−0.007*	−0.007*
	(0.004)	(0.003)	(0.004)	(0.003)
ATT20P	−0.000	−0.002	0.001	−0.001
	(0.001)	(0.001)	(0.001)	(0.001)
SERIESJ	−1.105**	−0.426**	−1.217**	0.253
	(0.190)	(0.151)	(0.470)	(0.381)
TIMEJ	0.374**	0.166+	1.207*	−0.118
	(0.123)	(0.098)	(0.572)	(0.446)
ALO1	−0.156	−0.367*	0.301	0.003
	(0.206)	(0.170)	(0.202)	(0.144)
ALO2	−0.104	−0.175	0.231	0.276+
	(0.204)	(0.169)	(0.203)	(0.148)
ALO3	−0.199	−0.363*	0.375+	−0.027
	(0.210)	(0.176)	(0.224)	(0.167)
ALOM	−0.845**	−0.585**	−0.334	−0.234
	(0.282)	(0.214)	(0.213)	(0.153)
HSNC86	−1.646**	−1.257**	−0.577**	−0.294*
	(0.099)	(0.089)	(0.170)	(0.118)
LSNC86	−1.272**	−0.798**	−0.580**	−0.188+
	(0.088)	(0.079)	(0.152)	(0.102)
COMBAT	−0.535**	−0.097	−0.187	−0.227
	(0.107)	(0.088)	(0.206)	(0.146)
COMSUP	−0.220*	0.067	−0.217+	−0.296**
	(0.112)	(0.095)	(0.128)	(0.098)
Dep mean:	0.885	0.770	0.802	0.708
R-square:	0.084	0.092	0.068	0.092
N =	9988	7433	3612	4910

NOTE: + = significant at the a = 0.10 confidence level.
    * = significant at the a = 0.05 confidence level.
  ** = significant at the a = 0.01 confidence level.

Table A.3

Logistic Regression Results for Duty Occupation Change During 15-Month Interval in FY86 Through FY87 in the Army National Guard and Army Reserve
(standard errors in parentheses)

Variable	Army National Guard		Army Reserve	
	NPS	PS	NPS	PS
INTERCEP	−2.221**	−2.302**	−2.328**	−2.447*
TIMEUN	−0.033	−0.001	0.069	0.033
	(0.030)	(0.029)	(0.049)	(0.034)
TIMEUN2	0.000	0.001	−0.005+	−0.001
	(0.001)	(0.002)	(0.003)	(0.002)
DIFFUN	0.245*	0.189+	0.096	0.078
	(0.121)	(0.112)	(0.167)	(0.130)
DIFFUNM	−0.363*	−0.034	−0.183	0.045
	(0.165)	(0.155)	(0.266)	(0.187)
YOS	−0.053**	−0.030+	−0.109**	−0.054*
	(0.020)	(0.017)	(0.034)	(0.025)
YOS2	0.001	0.001	0.003**	0.002
	(0.001)	(0.001)	(0.001)	(0.001)
PG4	−0.010	0.026	0.357*	0.094
	(0.108)	(0.250)	(0.155)	(0.258)
PG5	0.282*	0.041	0.797**	−0.010
	(0.136)	(0.251)	(0.194)	(0.266)
PG6	0.590**	−0.035	0.799**	0.171
	(0.174)	(0.262)	(0.256)	(0.280)
PG7	0.990**	0.549+	1.241**	0.549+
	(0.225)	(0.288)	(0.294)	(0.301)
PG8	4.085**	2.227**	2.777**	1.936**
	(0.303)	(0.356)	(0.361)	(0.344)
PG9	−0.110	−0.048	−0.007	−0.145
	(0.483)	(0.611)	(0.603)	(0.465)
FORMSERV	−0.010	−0.148*	−0.021	−0.137+
	(0.067)	(0.074)	(0.098)	(0.079)
OJTACT	−0.206*	0.069	0.219	0.016
	(0.093)	(0.087)	(0.144)	(0.095)
NHSG	0.209**	0.014	0.166	0.105
	(0.078)	(0.089)	(0.134)	(0.115)
HSPLUS	0.381**	0.133	0.186+	0.036
	(0.078)	(0.081)	(0.108)	(0.090)
CAT3	−0.097	−0.148+	−0.188+	−0.081
	(0.075)	(0.080)	(0.104)	(0.086)
CAT45	−0.323*	−0.191	−0.239	−0.216
	(0.138)	(0.170)	(0.164)	(0.142)

Table A.3—continued

Variable	Army National Guard		Army Reserve	
	NPS	PS	NPS	PS
CATM	0.019	−0.041		
	(0.134)	(0.105)		
SIZE100	0.270*	0.347*	0.711**	0.348**
	(0.126)	(0.138)	(0.159)	(0.124)
SIZE150	0.199	0.329*	0.618**	0.399**
	(0.126)	(0.138)	(0.165)	(0.133)
SIZE200	0.015	0.051	0.564**	0.496**
	(0.135)	(0.146)	(0.174)	(0.141)
SIZE200P	0.315+	0.413*	0.362*	0.321*
	(0.180)	(0.180)	(0.181)	(0.145)
ATT14	0.002	−0.000	−0.003	0.000
	(0.002)	(0.002)	(0.003)	(0.001)
ATT59	−0.001	0.001	0.004*	0.000
	(0.002)	(0.002)	(0.002)	(0.001)
ATT1019	−0.001	−0.000	0.006	−0.003
	(0.003)	(0.004)	(0.004)	(0.003)
ATT20P	−0.001	−0.000	0.002	0.003*
	(0.001)	(0.001)	(0.001)	(0.001)
SERIESJ	0.009	−0.274	−0.876+	−0.782+
	(0.182)	(0.176)	(0.498)	(0.447)
TIMEJ	−0.005	0.237*	1.121+	1.462**
	(0.118)	(0.114)	(0.610)	(0.524)
ALO1	−0.333+	0.025	0.114	0.047
	(0.191)	(0.198)	(0.211)	(0.168)
ALO2	−0.248	0.301	0.313	0.310+
	(0.190)	(0.196)	(0.212)	(0.171)
ALO3	−0.101	0.409*	0.523*	0.688**
	(0.196)	(0.205)	(0.235)	(0.193)
ALOM	−0.236	0.138	0.458*	0.896**
	(0.260)	(0.247)	(0.223)	(0.178)
HSNC86	0.293**	0.442**	−0.535**	0.197
	(0.095)	(0.105)	(0.178)	(0.138)
LSNC86	0.498**	0.288**	0.068	0.555**
	(0.084)	(0.093)	(0.159)	(0.119)
COMBAT	0.278**	0.093	−0.740**	−0.268
	(0.101)	(0.103)	(0.215)	(0.171)
COMSUP	0.202+	0.128	−0.159	0.051
	(0.105)	(0.111)	(0.134)	(0.115)
HD05	0.171	0.401**	0.324*	0.148
	(0.122)	(0.143)	(0.140)	(0.117)
HD550	0.276*	0.050	−0.092	−0.034
	(0.111)	(0.134)	(0.144)	(0.129)
HDGT50	0.412**	0.385+	0.140	0.435*

Table A.3—continued

Variable	Army National Guard		Army Reserve	
	NPS	PS	NPS	PS
	(0.154)	(0.202)	(0.211)	(0.192)
UD05	3.208**	3.002**	4.049**	3.650**
	(0.100)	(0.104)	(0.129)	(0.109)
UD550	3.258**	2.925**	2.737**	2.780**
	(0.170)	(0.170)	(0.253)	(0.202)
UDGT50	2.986**	3.164**	2.206**	2.444**
	(0.172)	(0.189)	(0.230)	(0.195)
CHPG	0.399**	0.216*	0.068	0.163
	(0.079)	(0.093)	(0.111)	(0.100)
DQUAL86	−1.107**	−1.179**	−0.877**	−0.808**
	(0.102)	(0.086)	(0.119)	(0.089)
Dep mean:	0.191	0.220	0.315	0.317
R-square:	0.221	0.228	0.315	0.298
N =	8809	6692	3344	4518

NOTE: + =   significant at the a = 0.10 confidence level.
    * =   significant at the a = 0.05 confidence level.
   ** =   significant at the a = 0.01 confidence level.

Table A.4

Logistic Regression Results for FY87 Duty Qualification of Job Changers During 15-Month Interval in FY86 Through FY87 in the Army National Guard and Army Reserve
(standard errors in parentheses)

Variable	Army National Guard		Army Reserve	
	NPS	PS	NPS	PS
INTERCEP	0.305**	−0.530**	−0.974**	−0.951**
YOS	−0.015	−0.033	0.033	−0.007
	(0.032)	(0.028)	(0.049)	(0.035)
YOS2	−0.000	0.001	−0.001	0.000
	(0.001)	(0.001)	(0.002)	(0.001)
PG4	0.318+	0.822*	−0.284	0.529
	(0.180)	(0.388)	(0.261)	(0.384)
PG5	0.245	0.802*	−0.033	0.531
	(0.211)	(0.390)	(0.307)	(0.399)
PG6	0.219	0.532	−0.242	0.460
	(0.273)	(0.414)	(0.431)	(0.425)
PG7	0.166	0.503	−0.126	0.763+
	(0.356)	(0.452)	(0.476)	(0.449)
PG8	1.572**	2.708**	1.245*	1.608**
	(0.388)	(0.498)	(0.541)	(0.487)
PG9	0.251	2.113+	−1.477	0.029
	(0.835)	(1.121)	(0.967)	(0.677)
NHSG	−0.009	−0.479**	0.258	0.039
	(0.148)	(0.163)	(0.229)	(0.195)
HSPLUS	0.113	0.001	0.313+	0.208
	(0.135)	(0.141)	(0.178)	(0.147)
CAT3	−0.177	0.169	0.028	−0.135
	(0.129)	(0.139)	(0.169)	(0.140)
CAT45	−0.249	0.290	0.201	−0.314
	(0.294)	(0.317)	(0.276)	(0.253)
CATM	−0.167	0.259		
	(0.226)	(0.176)		
HD05	−0.498*	0.282	−0.145	−0.200
	(0.200)	(0.213)	(0.223)	(0.183)
HD550	−0.036	−0.265	0.088	−0.242
	(0.191)	(0.229)	(0.248)	(0.220)
HDGT50	−0.065	−0.076	−0.062	−0.211
	(0.210)	(0.254)	(0.299)	(0.257)
UD05	−1.150**	−0.992**	−1.755**	−1.758**
	(0.154)	(0.160)	(0.209)	(0.171)
UD550	−0.670**	−0.399+	−0.861*	−1.002**
	(0.198)	(0.206)	(0.336)	(0.267)

Table A.4—continued

Variable	Army National Guard		Army Reserve	
	NPS	PS	NPS	PS
UDGT50	−0.909**	−0.616**	−1.178**	−0.560*
	(0.205)	(0.223)	(0.325)	(0.256)
CHPG	0.924**	1.057**	0.685**	0.731**
	(0.129)	(0.149)	(0.180)	(0.160)
DQUAL86	−0.846**	−0.598**	−0.058	−0.197
	(0.136)	(0.126)	(0.166)	(0.130)
NEWCOMP	−0.832**	−0.845**	0.566+	0.389
	(0.218)	(0.201)	(0.341)	(0.331)
REDESIGN	−0.444	−0.036	0.582	0.812*
	(0.305)	(0.320)	(0.535)	(0.407)
HSNC87	−0.001	0.118	1.320**	0.891**
	(0.201)	(0.192)	(0.248)	(0.202)
LSNC87	0.492**	0.241	0.503*	0.353*
	(0.171)	(0.162)	(0.206)	(0.167)
Dep mean:	0.416	0.399	0.354	0.338
R-square:	0.190	0.176	0.232	0.192
N =	1706	1500	1057	1439

NOTE: + = significant at the a = 0.10 confidence level.
      * = significant at the a = 0.05 confidence level.
     ** = significant at the a = 0.01 confidence level.

Table A.5

Logistic Regression Results for FY87 Duty Qualification of Qualified FY86 Reservists Not Changing Jobs in 15-Month Interval in the Army National Guard and Army Reserve (standard errors in parentheses)

Variable	Army National Guard		Army Reserve	
	NPS	PS	NPS	PS
INTERCEP	−0.129**	0.924**	−0.309**	−0.502**
YOS	−0.037	−0.110	−0.016	−0.060
	(0.052)	(0.034)	(0.096)	(0.045)
YOS2	−0.000	0.002	0.001	0.001
	(0.001)	(0.001)	(0.004)	(0.002)
PG4	0.813*	0.449	−0.073	0.348
	(0.331)	(0.514)	(0.403)	(0.418)
PG5	0.973*	0.362	−0.183	0.389
	(0.419)	(0.517)	(0.541)	(0.439)
PG6	0.702	0.347	−0.463	0.546
	(0.507)	(0.543)	(0.686)	(0.485)
PG7	0.784	0.569	−0.845	0.766
	(0.607)	(0.633)	(0.810)	(0.575)
PG8	0.644	−0.091	−0.394	0.617
	(1.018)	(0.787)	(0.993)	(0.667)
PG9	1.409	1.781	−0.016	2.331*
	(0.822)	(1.294)	(1.176)	(1.018)
NHSG	−0.420+	−0.129	0.105	−0.038
	(0.223)	(0.200)	(0.376)	(0.245)
HSPLUS	−0.500*	−0.449*	0.067	−0.049
	(0.209)	(0.170)	(0.275)	(0.185)
CAT3	−0.074	−0.038	−0.220	0.179
	(0.199)	(0.171)	(0.278)	(0.179)
CAT45	0.497	0.092	−0.956*	0.055
	(0.425)	(0.393)	(0.433)	(0.298)
CATM	−0.151	−0.226	0.333	
	(0.360)	(0.224)		
HD05	0.767*	0.274	0.415	0.333
	(0.333)	(0.280)	(0.370)	(0.231)
HD550	0.359	0.455	0.875*	−0.060
	(0.312)	(0.305)	(0.392)	(0.243)
HDGT50	−0.080	−0.684	−0.596	0.327
	(0.411)	(0.489)	(0.651)	(0.440)
UD05	0.182	−0.053	0.695	0.088
	(0.257)	(0.234)	(0.506)	(0.333)
UD550	−0.497	0.117	2.174*	0.861
	(0.451)	(0.398)	(1.130)	(0.607)

Table A.5—continued

Variable	Army National Guard		Army Reserve	
	NPS	PS	NPS	PS
UDGT50	−0.547	0.266	0.239	0.151
	(0.420)	(0.487)	(0.699)	(0.487)
CHPG	1.496**	1.552**	1.134**	1.028**
	(0.248)	(0.235)	(0.289)	(0.199)
NEWCOMP	0.305	−0.590	0.471	
	(0.748)	(0.692)	(0.803)	
REDESIGN	−0.050	−1.022*	−0.788	0.342
	(0.834)	(0.580)	(0.914)	(0.847)
HSNC87	−0.275	−0.871**	−0.237	−0.076
	(0.282)	(0.234)	(0.483)	(0.263)
HSNC87	−0.064	−0.297	0.026	−0.036
	(0.264)	(0.218)	(0.428)	(0.232)
Dep mean:	0.555	0.565	0.452	0.499
R-square:	.112	.135	.130	.064
N =	654	926	332	696

NOTE: + =   significant at the a = 0.10 confidence level.
      * =   significant at the a = 0.05 confidence level.
     ** =   significant at the a = 0.01 confidence level.

REFERENCES

Defense Manpower Data Center, *The 1986 Reserve Components Surveys,* 1987.

Grissmer, David W., Richard Buddin, and Sheila Nataraj Kirby, *Improving Reserve Compensation: A Review of Current Compensation and Related Personnel and Training-Readiness Issues,* RAND, R-3707-FMP/RA, September 1989.

Lee, L. F., "Fully Recursive Probability Models and Multivariate Log-Linear Probability Models for the Analysis of Qualitative Data," *Journal of Econometrics,* Vol. 16, 1981, pp. 51–69.

Maddala, G., *Limited Dependent and Qualitative Variables in Econometrics,* Cambridge University Press, Cambridge, England, 1983.

Schmidt, P., and R. Strauss, "Estimation of Models with Jointly Dependent Qualitative Variables: A Simultaneous Logit Approach," *Econometrica,* Vol. 43, No. 4, 1975, pp. 745–755.